Praise for Modern-Day Vikings

Sweden is arguably the most American country in Europe. Even so, the cultural differences between us are more profound and more subtle than what is apparent to the casual visitor. Christina Robinowitz and Lisa Werner Carr have produced an excellent—and highly entertaining—guide for those who wish to understand [Swedes] and who, at the same time, are anxious not to put their foot in it.

—Olle Wästberg
Consul General of Sweden in New York,
former editor-in-chief of *Expressen* Newspaper

[Modern-Day Vikings] is wonderful—balanced, well researched [and] beautifully written.... [It's] an invaluable resource for Swedes and Americans who need to interact for...social, educational or genealogical purposes; [for] traveling or business-oriented pursuits.

—Carrin Patman,
Chairman of the Steering Committee for an Endowment in
Swedish Studies, University of Texas

This practical book is a must-have for all businessmen and -women involved in Swedish-American trade relations. The authors present the topic in a straightforward manner, giving everybody interested in intercultural matters an amusing and rewarding experience.

—Bo Hedfors
Executive Vice President, Motorola

At a time when Swedish IT entrepreneurs are conquering the world, Modern-Day Vikings provides an excellent guide to Swedish business behavior, set against a historical background. Useful

D0050088

hints are given on how to avoid disastrous misunderstandings. Also, for Swedes, the book gives interesting historical explanations [as] to why we behave as we do.

—Cecilia Julin
Minister for Economic Affairs
Swedish Embassy, Washington, D.C.

The authors really hit the nail on the head! I will certainly buy this book for my American husband, my children and my close American friends. After reading [Modern-Day Vikings] they will know exactly where this Swede is coming from. The book is a refresher course in Swedish history and filled with many good laughs.

—Kerstin Nordqvist Lane
Consul for Sweden, Chicago
Executive Director, Swedish American Museum, Chicago

Swedes can sometimes be an enigma even to themselves. Authors Werner Carr and Robinowitz, with their very different backgrounds, offer a key to common and not-so-common differences between those things Swedish and the world. Modern-Day Vikings could become mandatory for those with an interest in, or plans to work with or in Sweden, but is also quite amusing and an eye opener for us born Swedes.

—Ulf Mårtensson
editor & publisher, *Swedish News,*
Sweden & America Magazine and Nordstjernan

From…the opening paragraphs to the comprehensive bibliography, [Modern-Day Vikings] is well researched and well written. As a Swedish manager, I say: This book accurately describes the Swedes and provides very useful information regarding how to interact with them. Were I an American manager I'd say: This book is a must for anyone doing business with Swedes and going about it seriously!

—Göran Fröling
Vice President and General Manager, Ericsson Canada

MODERN-DAY
VIKINGS

INTERCULTURAL PRESS
A Nicholas Brealey Publishing Company

BOSTON • LONDON

The InterAct Series

Christina Johansson Robinowitz is available as consultant, trainer and speaker on the subjects covered in this book. She can be reached at The Cross-Cultural Coach—Intercultural Services
Phone: 214-363-2853
e-mail: crobinowitz@culturalcoach.com
www.culturalcoach.com

Lisa Werner Carr is a professional writer based in Dallas, Texas. She can be reached at lisa.carr@reporters.net

MODERN-DAY

VIKINGS

A Practical Guide to Interacting with the Swedes

Christina Johansson Robinowitz
and
Lisa Werner Carr

First published by Intercultural Press, a Nicholas Brealey
Publishing company. For more information, contact:

Intercultural Press, Inc.   Nicholas Brealey Publishing
A division of   3–5 Spafield Street
Nicholas Brealey Publishing   Clerkenwell
53 State Street, 9th Floor   London, EC1R 4QB, UK
Boston, MA 02109, USA   Tel: (+) 44-207-239-0360
Tel: (+) 617-523-3801   Fax: (+) 44-207-239-0370
Fax: (+) 617-523-3708

www.nicholasbrealey.com

©2001 by Christina Johansson Robinowitz and Lisa Werner Carr

Production and cover design by Patty J. Topel

All rights reserved. No part of this publication may be reproduced
in any manner whatsoever without written permission from the
publisher, except in the case of brief quotations embodied in critical articles or reviews.

Printed in the United States of America

19 18 17 16   11 12 13 14 15

Library of Congress Cataloging-in-Publication Data

Robinowitz, Christina Johansson.
    Modern-day Vikings: a practical guide to interacting with the
Swedes / Christina Johansson Robinowitz and Lisa Werner Carr.
       p.   cm.
    Includes bibliographical references and index.
    ISBN 1-877864-88-9 (alk. paper)
       1. National characteristics, Swedish.   2. Sweden—Social
life and customs—20th century.   3. Sweden—History.
I. Carr, Lisa Werner.   II. Title.
DS639.R63 2001
306'.09485   2001039914

Dedication

To my children, Anna and Andy, who taught me the value of seeing life from more than one perspective.

—Christina

To my husband, Tom Carr, for his indefatigable support and unconditional love.

—Lisa

Table of Contents

Acknowledgments

We would first like to extend a special thanks to Judy Carl-Hendrick, our editor at Intercultural Press, who guided us through the process of producing this book with good humor and a lot of patience. We would like to thank the following gentlemen with (or formerly with) Ericsson, Inc., for sharing their insights on doing business in Sweden and the United States: Bo Hedfors, Gary Pinkham, Mark Broms, Kjell Wallin, and Jan Henriques. We are grateful to the managers and employees at Nolato Texas and Nolato Shieldmate for allowing us to follow developments in their multicultural workplace. We also appreciated the opportunity to speak with Lyndon L. Olson Jr., former U.S. ambassador to Sweden, and Magnus Moliteus, former director of the Invest in Sweden Agency.

The following individuals also deserve special recognition: Lasse Sjöberg and Kerstin Brandelius-Johansson, for diligently promoting Swedish-American business relationships; Kerstin and Mårten Broddheimer, for acting as excellent sounding boards; Tommy Möller, assistant professor of political science xiv

at Stockholm University, for sharing his wealth of expertise; and journalist and photographer Tommy Olsson, for generously reviewing draft after draft and offering improvements tirelessly.

Many other people provided invaluable insights and information along the way, including Laila Andersson, Robin Battison, Marc Bünger, Kathey and Russell Carreiro, Kirk Chilton, Tom Connor, David Curle, Kerstin Lane, Anders Lindkvist, Ulf Mårtensson, Lena Olofsson-Piras, Dan Olson, Brian Palmer, Pernilla and Johan Schoug, Sven Sedin, Judee Shuler, Myleen Sjödin, Suzanne Southard, John Steinberg, David Trouba, Olle Wästberg, and Lena Zander. For others too numerous to mention, including family and friends, we express our sincere appreciation and gratitude.

Introduction

September 3, 1967, was a watershed day in the history of
Sweden, not for what happened, but for what didn't happen.
That day at 5:00 A.M., Swedish automobile drivers switched
from driving on the left side of the road, as the British do, to
driving on the right—and they did so without incident. No
accidents were reported. The Swedes calmly took the change in
stride, bemused by the attention the nonevent received abroad.

That such a major shift took place with remarkable equa-
nimity exemplifies in many ways how the people of Sweden
view the world: anything can be accomplished in an orderly
fashion when everyone cooperates. But the philosophy has a
corollary: life can be difficult for those who do not "cooper-
ate"—which may simply mean not agreeing with the majority
or consensus view. Sometimes too much agreement impedes
creativity and the search for new ideas.

On the surface, the Swedish and American cultures appear
quite similar. Most Swedes speak good English and consider
themselves very knowledgeable about all things American.
More than two million Americans count themselves as descendants of Swedish immigrants and believe that they understand their cultural heritage. The countries share a taste
for popular culture and an interest in high technology, particularly telecommunications and the Internet.

These similarities, however, conceal essential differences that become apparent when Swedes and Americans interact, either socially or in the workplace. Americans often find Swedes difficult to communicate with, and many Americans living in Sweden initially feel isolated and confused by a culture that outwardly appears to be like their own, yet upon closer examination reveals itself to be so different.

This book explores those aspects of the Swedish culture that reveal specific Swedish beliefs, values, attitudes, and behavior. We begin with a historical overview that explains how some typically Swedish traits have roots extending back to Viking times. We look at Sweden's well-known model of "cradle-to-grave" social democracy, at the economic and social changes currently taking place in Sweden, and at how the nation developed. We study the underlying values of the modern Swedish people, many of which, such as the concepts of *lagom* (moderation) and the Law of Jante (personal modesty), are very unlike those held in the United States. We also explore other common Swedish characteristics such as the importance of self-sufficiency and the fear of looking foolish.

Finally, we look at the Swedes' communication style, customs and etiquette, and important cultural traits related to doing business in Sweden—the discouragement of individual competition and the role of consensus-based decision making.

As with most cultures, certain stereotypes about Swedes have emerged, some based at least in small part on fact. However, many beliefs about Swedes are unfounded, such as the alleged high Swedish suicide rate or their obsession with sex. Understanding how these images have developed and the values underlying them will help you interact with Swedes in the United States or Sweden in a positive and effective way. We wish you a *trevlig resa*—a pleasant journey—on your way to learning more about the Swedes and their culture.

—Christina Johansson Robinowitz
and Lisa Werner Carr

1

From the Vikings to the Welfare State: A Millennium in Sweden

*Praise no day until evening, no wife until buried, no sword until tested, no maid until bedded, no ice until crossed, no ale until drunk.**

—*Hávamál*

Could a ninth-century admonition against jumping to conclusions really carry any weight in the twenty-first century? The answer is yes; a modern Swede is still likely to agree with the spirit set forth by these words from the *Hávamál*, part of the poetic *Edda* of Viking lore. Many non-Swedes, particularly Americans, have found Swedes to be extremely cautious. The Swedes, on the other hand, consider their behavior nothing more than rational and sensible—pragmatic qualities that they value highly.

This sense of caution is exemplary of a characteristic of the Swedes today that originates in their distant past. The Swedes' modern history alone stretches back more than a millennium, making for plenty of cultural baggage as well as treasures.

In this chapter, we present an overview of Swedish history from the pre-Vikings to the conception of the welfare state,

---

* Note: all translations are by the authors unless otherwise specified.

1

2

with the aim of establishing the foundation for the cultural exploration to follow. Cultural values such as independence, equality, and cooperation don't develop overnight, or even over a century. To really begin to understand the Swedes, you have to dig much, much deeper.

The Viking Age: Prehistory to 1050

Scandinavia as we know it today is composed of three countries: Sweden, Denmark, and Norway.[†] Many non-Swedes think that Sweden's history began with the Vikings, but archeological finds dating from the Stone Age to the Iron Age reveal that Sweden's earliest inhabitants appeared about eight thousand to ten thousand years ago, trailing the glaciers that were receding northward up the Scandinavian peninsula.

The ancestors of today's Swedes were hunter-gatherers and fishers. They used the sea and the country's numerous lakes and rivers to travel and trade throughout their region and, later, the world. An agrarian society developed as climatic changes made it easier to work the soil. By the time the Viking culture emerged, the people of the region were farmers. They cultivated grain and vegetables during the short summer season and raised livestock. Around A.D. 500, the settlements near Lake Mälaren, outside present-day Stockholm, emerged as the seat of power for the tribe known as the Sveas—the group for which Sweden was later named: *Sverige* (realm of the Sveas).

The historical era remembered as the "Viking Age" was a concentrated period of exploration, commerce, combat, and colonization by the people of Scandinavia that lasted about three hundred years, from 790 to 1066.

Scandinavia at that time was not yet divided into the freestanding nations of Denmark, Norway, and Sweden; people lived in autonomous tribes led by local kings or chief-

---

[†] Finland is often included within Scandinavia, but it is actually of a different ethnic heritage.

tains. Collectively, however, chroniclers on the continent referred to them as the *Northmen*, or the Norse (hence Nordic). Throughout the period these people spoke a mutually intelligible Germanic language known today as Old Norse. Not all Norse were Vikings. Vikings were local chieftains, warriors, or other prominent men who periodically left their farms and settlements seeking adventure, trade, and plunder. A chieftain often enlisted other men to serve on his ship for a voyage that could last months or even years in exchange for a share of the profits. Many who left never returned; others returned with tales and treasure.

So what made farmers into marauders? To go "viking" was a way to make a living combining piracy, trade, and colonization. "In an agrarian world they needed land for their children and grass for their stock; in an era of opening trade routes, they craved silver and the chattels that silver could provide; in a hierarchical, warlike, and still partly tribal society, their leaders sought fame, power, wealth, and sustenance through action" (Jones 1984, 2).

The origin of the word *Viking* is still debated. Many historians believe it comes from the Norse *vík*, meaning "bay, fjord, or creek"; thus a Viking was one who sailed from or lurked in a *vík*. Others point to the Norse verb *víkja*, which meant to move fast or to recede into the distance—an interpretation many communities looted by the Vikings would certainly understand (Jones 1984, 76). Some confusion stems from the fact that historical sources often use the words *Norse* and *Viking* interchangeably to describe the barbarians from the north.

For the most part raiding proved easier than trading. The Vikings of western Scandinavia launched three centuries of terror with the raid on the English monastery of Lindisfarne in 793. The isolated monasteries of the British Isles were not only extremely wealthy but also poorly defended. Priests didn't fight back, making them easy targets for hit-and-run attacks. "Deliver us, O Lord, from the fury of the Norsemen" became part of the common English prayer.

The Norse were outstanding shipbuilders, and the Vikings took to the sea and rivers in their multioared dragon boats to explore every corner of Europe, and often beyond. The Vikings used their ships to make regular raids on their favorite victims. In some cases they demanded protection money in lieu of attack; other times they plundered wildly and at will, killing anyone who resisted and providing inspiration for the English word *berserk*.

Underlying the Vikings' fearlessness in battle was the pagan Norse faith known as Asa, which scorned fear of death. Indeed, dying in battle ensured entry to Valhalla, the Vikings' afterworld paradise. And warriors knew their heroic deeds would likely be commemorated by their survivors, carved (using the runic alphabet) into slabs of stone, rune stones that can still be found across Scandinavia one thousand years later, or regaled in the poetic verses of *skalds*, or poets.

As opposed to the Vikings of western Scandinavia, the Vikings of Sweden took little part in the raids on Britain, although they could be just as violent. Instead, their ambitions took them eastward. Swedish merchants and marauders traveled the Volga River into the interior of Eastern Europe, establishing trading posts at Riga, Novgorod, and Kiev. Known as the "Rus"—referring to the travelers' fair, ruddy complexions or coming from the Finnish word for Sweden, *Ruotsi*, depending on the expert one asks—they gave their name to a nation they are credited with founding: Russia. From Kiev, the Swedish Vikings attacked Constantinople so relentlessly that the authorities there eventually gave in and hired them as bodyguards, thus opening a permanent trade route between Russia and the Byzantine Empire.

The Swedes traveled eastward to the Aral and Caspian Seas and were thus exposed to trade goods from as far away as China, and south to Baghdad and the Mediterranean. As a result, Persian glass, Chinese silk, wine and exotic spices, and silver coins and jewelry made their way to Sweden, acquired in exchange for weapons, amber, honey, wax, fur, and even slaves.[‡] That brings us to the third element of Viking culture: colonization. Some of the Vikings who came to foreign lands to trade or raid decided to stay, their temporary camps becoming permanent settlements. During the late eighth century, Norwegian Vikings colonized the Scottish Islands, the Isle of Man, and Ireland; in the ninth century, fleeing political unrest, a group of them moved on to populate Iceland. During the tenth century, nearly half of England lay under the domination of Danish Vikings. Many Finns, Russians, and Ukrainians today count Swedish Vikings among their ancestors.

Bloodlust aside, Norse society was ahead of its time in many ways. The Vikings who settled Iceland founded the world's first democratic assembly, the Althing, in 930. When the men were at sea, women were in charge at home. A husband would literally turn the keys to the farm over to his wife when he left, making her responsible for managing it. As a result, Norse women had greater freedom and authority than was customary at this time in other cultures. Norse women could own and inherit property and were free to divorce.

Because each of them had a stake in the voyage's success, the Vikings were surprisingly egalitarian aboard ship. One tale relates that when the prince of the Franks sent an envoy to bargain with the chief of a group of Viking raiders approaching Paris, the envoy returned perplexed. "I found no one to talk with," he explained. "They said they were all chiefs" (Vesilind 2000, 9).

[‡] It often goes unmentioned that the Vikings often captured, kept, and sold vanquished enemies as slaves, or thralls. But it was an equal opportunity industry: they could be enslaved themselves, should they end up on the losing side of the battle. Viking slaves were highly prized as rowers and soldiers.

Today's Swedish banker, teacher, or engineer is unlikely to be mistaken for an axe-wielding Viking, but he or she may still share some of the traits that made the Vikings successful, such as an attitude of individual integrity combined with a willingness to work toward a common goal. As the opening phrase from the *Hávamál* suggests, the Viking will not judge the success of his journey until he has returned home safely with a shipload of treasures. Nor will his descendants jump to conclusions, but instead demand ample evidence.

The Middle Ages: 1066–1500

As noted previously, the Norse were not a Christian people during the Viking era, but they were religious. Their faith was strongly rooted in the worship of powerful gods, including Odin, god of war; Thor, god of thunder; and Frey, god of fertility—for whom Wednesday, Thursday, and Friday are named, respectively. Human and animal sacrifices were made on their behalf and prayers offered to them to ensure the success of every venture.

The Scandinavians were slow to accept Christianity, and the Swedes were the last Germanic people to officially adopt it. Because they were a "heathen" people, the Vikings' nastiness was sometimes blamed on their religion—priests were shocked that the raiders had "no respect for the sanctity of religious houses and the pacifism of their inmates" (Jones 1984, 132). It is more likely, however, that the Vikings targeted churches and monasteries for their wealth, as described above, rather than for religious purposes.

The first Christian missionary, Ansgar, successfully established a church in the Viking stronghold of Birka in the ninth century, but the murder of a later missionary in 936 sent the Christians packing. By the time the Viking Age came to a close, however, Christianity was at last making inroads into Sweden. The first Christian Swedish king was baptized in 1000, although it took another 150 years for the faith to really take hold. Paganism continued openly until the 1120s (Jones and Pennick 1995, 137).

In 1210 a union between church and state was formed that remained until 2000, when the Lutheran Church of Sweden and the government finally and officially separated. Until that time, every Swedish citizen was counted as a member of the Church of Sweden unless he or she specified otherwise. It was the influence of the church that brought Sweden into the "civilized" European fold. In the 1200s, the country wrote down its laws for the first time. Slavery was abolished in 1355 because of church teachings stating that all men are equal in the eyes of God.[§] The church grew quite powerful, acquiring vast tracts of land and establishing itself in the city of Uppsala, just miles from the site where Viking kings were crowned and buried.

At the end of the Viking era and into the early Middle Ages, a nobility began to emerge in the area now known as Sweden. Feuding among and within various dynasties was frequent as the families of Christian King Erik and his rival Sverker fought for control of the emerging nation.

At the same time, Sweden vied with its neighbors for control of the Baltic Sea. The Baltic had become increasingly important with the expansion and growing influence of the German Hanseatic League, based in Lübeck. Sweden had had a presence in Finland since the Viking days, but the Russian region of Novgorod was interested in a stake of its own. In 1323 Sweden and Russia signed a treaty dividing control of Finland, thus linking its destiny with that of both Sweden and Russia for the next six hundred years and beyond. Sections of western Finland remain Swedish-speaking, and Swedish is Finland's second official language.

[§] It is also relevant to note that Sweden was one of the few countries in medieval Europe where feudalism did not take hold; the Swedes were never serfs. The preponderance of independent farmers helped to minimize social class differences and nurtured an ethic of equality.

By the end of the fourteenth century, the Scandinavians had tired of German domination of trade. In 1397 Sweden, Norway, and Denmark formed the Union of Kalmar in an attempt to team up against the Germans. It was the only time in history when these three nations were ruled under one crown, that of Queen Margareta of Denmark. The union was successful at keeping the Germans at bay, but the alliance was a loose and uneasy one. Although Denmark dominated the union, the infighting was ferocious. On one side, there was conflict between the monarchy and the nobility; on the other, peasants and merchants constantly threatened rebellion. In 1434 a Swedish nobleman attempted to seize power in Stockholm. He was killed, but his nationalism survived and began to spread. Border skirmishes against the Danes became more frequent and were often secretly backed by the Hanseatic League.

The Foundation of Sweden: 1500–1600

The Union of Kalmar officially persisted, but by 1500 the Swedish nobles openly demanded more power and autonomy from Denmark. They had already formed a national assembly, the first step toward self-rule. In 1520 they voted to burn down the fortress of the pro-Danish Roman Catholic archbishop of Sweden, a nobleman named Gustav Trolle (who himself was imprisoned).

Danish King Christian II now had an excuse to act. He traveled to Stockholm, where the merchants, desperate to save their city from destruction, opened their doors to him. Christian II responded by inviting the noblemen of Stockholm to a banquet. At the end of this feast, however, he ordered all of those who had opposed him beheaded. More than eighty noblemen were murdered in what came to be known as the "Stockholm Bloodbath."

One young nobleman to escape this fate was Gustav Vasa. While his father, two uncles, and brother-in-law were being killed, he was in Denmark, a hostage of King Christian II. Vasa managed to escape captivity and flee back to Sweden, where he traveled the country to elicit support to overthrow the Danes, but his efforts were unsuccessful. Discouraged, he set out on skis for Norway to win help there. By then, however, news of the Stockholm Bloodbath had reached the Swedish region of Dalarna, where the people had long been unhappy under Danish rule. The people of Dalarna sent their two fastest skiers to catch Vasa and bring him back to lead a successful revolt. This event is commemorated each year in a ski race called Vasaloppet.

In 1523, Gustav Vasa, often called the "Father of Sweden," was crowned king of Sweden, and the Union of Kalmar came to an end. Considered an enlightened ruler, Vasa brought about far-reaching reforms during his thirty-seven-year reign. He centralized power in Sweden and established a hereditary monarchy. He reorganized the government, the monetary system, and the army. Refused papal recognition of his reign, he supported the Swedish Reformation to Lutheranism that was already under way. He had debts to pay: defeating Christian II had been expensive, and he still had conflicts to settle among the remaining noblemen. But like his Viking forefathers, he knew where the money was: he confiscated the property of the Roman Catholic Church in Sweden.

What happened to Norway after Sweden broke away from the Union of Kalmar? It remained under the thumb of its more powerful Danish neighbors. Denmark would retain control of what is today southern Sweden until 1658 and remain united with Norway until 1817.[II]

[II] In 1814 Norway was ceded to Sweden but would become independent and separate under the Swedish crown. This union continued until 1905, when it was dissolved—with some tension but without war.

Sweden as a World Power: 1618–1717

Sweden, a major superpower? Most Americans are unaware that like many other European countries, Sweden also took a turn as a great imperialist nation. This period began with the ascent to the throne in 1611 of King Gustav II Adolf (also known as Gustavus Adolphus), a grandson of Gustav Vasa and a military genius. He brought his grandfather's talent and enthusiasm to the task of strengthening Sweden's position in Europe.

Sweden's military expansion began with its participation in the misnamed Thirty Years' War, which started in 1630. The war eventually led to Sweden's conquest of most of the Baltic States, including huge territories as far away as Poland. (One of the king's dreams was to make the Baltic "a Swedish lake.") Sweden was double its current size. Gustaf II Adolf developed Sweden's military capabilities by exploiting one of the country's greatest natural resources, iron, to produce rifles and cannons; by developing an organized education system; and by introducing the first conscript army.

One notable stain on Gustaf II Adolf's otherwise immaculate record was the scandal of the warship *Vasa*. Built to be the pride of the Swedish navy, it sank ignominiously beneath the waters of Stockholm harbor moments after its launch in 1628. More than one hundred seamen perished. Modern analysts blame the sinking on a faulty design allowing for too many cannons on deck, making the ship top-heavy. The *Vasa* remained submerged in the cold, brackish Baltic waters until 1961, when a team of conservationists raised the vessel. Surprisingly well preserved, the *Vasa* was painstakingly restored and can now be seen at Stockholm's modern Vasa Museum.

King Gustaf II Adolf died on the battlefield in 1632 and was succeeded by his six-year-old daughter Kristina, the first female to occupy the Swedish throne. The king's former chancellor continued to implement the king's policies and expansion during Kristina's childhood. When she came of age, Queen

Kristina reigned over one of the most opulent and beautiful courts in Europe and was considered a remarkably gifted and intelligent woman. In a move that stunned her loyal subjects, however, she abdicated her reign in 1654 to move to Rome and convert to Roman Catholicism—an outrage to a nation that had fought so long against Catholic countries.[§]

The beginning of the end for Sweden's days as a great power came with the reign of King Karl XII, who is, ironically, remembered by many Swedes as a heroic, romantic warrior figure. Although he was also considered a military genius by many, he fought the Russians, the Poles, and the Danes with both success and failure. By the time he died in 1718, allegedly of a gold bullet to the brain (it was widely believed that a normal bullet could not kill him), he had lost all the territories Sweden had won, save Finland (which it would lose to Russia in 1809 during the Napoleonic Wars) and Pomerania (a piece of modern-day Poland that it lost to Denmark in 1814). Yet he continues to be admired by rightist and nationalist groups in Sweden alike, who have made him a bizarre symbol of their often violent ideologies.

The Age of Enlightenment: The 1700s

The eighteenth century witnessed the blossoming of science, the arts, and philosophy across Europe. A number of brilliant Swedish scientists and thinkers came to the fore, including naturalist Carl von Linné (or Linnaeus) and scientist-philosopher Emanuel Swedenborg. And in Gustav III, who came to power in 1772, the Swedes had a king who was dedicated to advancing the nation's arts and sciences.

Greatly influenced by the French culture, which was dominant at the time, Gustav III built Stockholm's Royal Opera House and introduced the stage to Swedish culture by constructing Stockholm's Dramatic Theatre and hiring Swedish

---

[§] Sweden subsequently changed its laws of succession to prevent women from assuming the throne, a law it retained until 1979.

actors and playwrights for the theatre of Drottningholm Palace. He commissioned the first opera written in Swedish. He created the Swedish Academy of Literature (a group modeled on the French Academy) that is famous today for awarding the Nobel Prize for Literature each year. Gustav III also founded the nation's musical academy and academy of art. A number of writers and composers emerged during this period, including troubadour Carl-Michael Bellman (whom we will take up in chapter 4 on national pride).

But his activities were not limited to the arts. During his reign, many restrictions on free trade were lifted and religious freedom was extended to foreigners in the country. Not surprisingly, the king became very popular with his subjects.

Not everyone was happy, however. The power struggle between the Swedish nobility and the monarchy that was launched during the Middle Ages with the reign of Gustav Vasa had persisted. Gustav III once again antagonized the aristocracy with his demand for absolute power. In the end he went too far and was assassinated by his enemies at a masked ball. Gustav III lives on in the opera *The Masked Ball* by Giuseppe Verdi, which reenacts the assassination. The king would have been pleased.

A Fresh Start for Sweden: The 1800s

The last of the Vasas to rule Sweden was Gustav III's son, Gustav IV Adolf. His main contribution to the nation was land reform; it ended the practice, which had long been problematic, of dividing land into smaller and smaller plots as it passed from generation to generation. Instead, larger farming units were created and the land reparceled out to farmers.*

---

* The land redistribution solved some problems but created others; while it consolidated arable land, it also had the effect of moving farmers from the towns where they congregated and lived out into the country, making them more socially isolated.

He also led Sweden into its last war. During France's Reign of Terror, Gustaf IV Adolf launched a campaign against France, putting him at odds with France's ally, Russia. Russia promptly invaded Finland, still ruled by Sweden. When the dust settled in 1809, Sweden's modern border had been established. It had lost a third of its territory, including Finland and part of northern Sweden. The nobility had had enough. Gustav IV Adolf abdicated and Sweden made peace with its neighbors.

Jean-Baptiste Bernadotte, a French general who had been successful and popular in Napoleon Bonaparte's army, was recruited in 1809 to be Sweden's new king and assumed the throne in 1818 (we'll meet him again when we discuss equality in Sweden). A new constitution was adopted, distributing the power of the state among the king, Parliament, and Council. Sweden became a constitutional monarchy, which it remains today. With it, the country embarked on a policy of nonalignment with other nations in peacetime and neutrality in war.

During the nineteenth century, Sweden began to progress in other areas as well. Population growth, which had been slow because of high mortality rates, especially infant mortality, boomed in the nineteenth century; the population grew from 2.4 million in the early 1800s to 5.1 million by the early 1900s. The increase was primarily due to medical improvements such as smallpox vaccinations, more plentiful and better food from more efficient farming, and improved hygiene in general. The formula, according to the Swedish poet Esias Tegner, was "peace, vaccination and potatoes."

While the sudden population growth helped Sweden progress, it also had an unintended effect: not enough cultivatable land was available to sustain the growth. In order to keep land in a family, a common practice allowed the oldest son to inherit it undivided; subsequent children received nothing. This created a growing underclass and led to mass emigration, primarily to "Amerika," where land was reputed to be in abundance. In the 1880s alone, almost 350,000 emigrants left Sweden, and between 1865 and 1914 the total was close to one million.**

Making Connections

We take our histories with us, wherever we go. The Vikings' sense of democracy and egalitarianism within the group live on in modern Sweden. Swedish women today pride themselves on self-sufficiency and independence and are not likely to accept a subservient role on the job or at home. A foreign businessperson, confronted with Sweden's flat management style, could ask to talk to the boss and receive a response frustratingly similar to the one the Frankish envoy received on the Viking vessel: "We are all chiefs." Rather than a collective society, Sweden is one of like-minded individuals, working together.

The solidarity forged under the Swedes' revolt against the Danes under Gustav Vasa reemerged in the struggle of the Swedish union movement to attain better working conditions and a measure of equality in the late nineteenth century. As a result of this struggle to level the hierarchy, labor and management in Sweden have created a working relationship seen nowhere else (to the relief of employers in the United States, among others).

Other aspects from Sweden's past have been left behind. Unlike countries such as France or England, which still recall their days of "greatness" with nostalgia, Sweden is unlikely to wax poetic on its days of military glory, however grand. This is less a reflection of the period's historical significance than of the attitude of today's Swedes. If anything, Swedes are

---

** Often overlooked is the fact that some 200,000 emigrants eventually returned to Sweden, bringing with them the energy and industry to found political parties, social movements, and successful companies.

more proud of the fact that their country has not been at war in nearly two hundred years than they are of former glory. Despite centuries of bitter warfare, surprisingly little rancor exists among the Scandinavian countries today, particularly compared with hot spots such as the Balkans. Certainly, touchy issues remain; for example, Sweden's position of neutrality during World War II put the country in the position of not defending its neighbors against German invasion. This was not forgotten in Norway and Denmark and caused animosity in the past, but the nations have put the past behind them.

Some rivalry also stems from Sweden's social and political successes in the twentieth century, which we will read about in the next chapter. Sweden can come across as quite a know-it-all in these areas. Sweden is also about twice the size in population of Denmark, Norway, and Finland. Just as the United States is in many ways admired but also resented at times because of its size and power, so Sweden can sometimes be perceived as the annoying "big brother." Nonetheless, Scandinavians today are more likely to stress their similarities than their differences and to emphasize the challenge of their collective future over the troubles of the past.

Chapter 2 will look at how Sweden dealt with some of the growing pains of the recent past with the development of the Swedish Model, the country's cradle-to-grave system of social welfare, and some of the challenges that model faces as it enters its second century.

2

The Rise of the Swedish Model

En sällsynt ros som blommar bara på en enda plats och under
speciella omständigheter. *(A rare rose that blooms only in one
place and under very special circumstances.)*
— The Swedish welfare system described
during a 1995 debate in Paris

Summary: A desire to improve working and living conditions
for the Swedish working class following the country's entry
into the Industrial Revolution gave rise to the Swedish Model.
The Social Democratic Party emerged to lead and organize
workers in a movement for greater equality and fairness, and
the power of labor unions grew under the party's influence.
After a rocky start labor and employers were able to hammer
out guidelines for collective bargaining and thus mutual cooperation.

In order to understand modern Sweden, one must understand
the country's unique sociopolitical system, known worldwide
as the Swedish Model. During the twentieth century, Sweden
became world-renowned for its "prosperous, democratic welfare state, its wealth created by a vigorous private sector, but
distributed in accordance with an egalitarian vision of social
justice" (Board 1995, 1).

Although some Swedes have become cynical about the future of the welfare state, most continue to support its original aims. By looking at the history and values that underlie the Swedish Model, the political party that developed it, and the social and economic factors that now challenge it, you will be able to better understand the concepts discussed in this book.

The History

With no national railroad until the 1870s, Sweden was a latecomer to the Industrial Revolution, but once the revolution began, the country made a swift transition from an agricultural to an industrial society. Railroads facilitated use of the country's natural resources of timber, steel, and iron and exportation of goods such as glass and textiles. The 1890s witnessed the founding of some of Sweden's major industrial companies, which fueled the migration of large numbers of former farmworkers to Sweden's cities, particularly Stockholm. By the end of the nineteenth century, only 50 percent of the population made a living on the farm, compared with 90 percent just decades before.

Most newcomers found jobs in factories, but few found the prosperity they sought. Working and living conditions were frequently bad and while industrialists became rich, most people remained poor. Under these conditions demand for greater equality and fairness grew. Traditional Swedish society, with its marked differences in social class, became a target for change, and reformers sought to abolish class differences altogether.

Sweden's modern union movement was launched in 1879 with a major strike in the north-central town of Sundsvall. From then on, Swedish workers began organizing to seek better conditions for the working class. Employers fought the movement initially, even using force to stop union organizers.

In 1889 the labor movement led to the foundation of the Social Democratic Party. In his autobiography former Swedish Prime Minister Tage Erlander, a Social Democrat and the longest-serving prime minister in Swedish history, stated that something was wrong "with a social system where the country's most fertile land is owned by the richest people, but farmed by the poorest."

Through the influence of the Social Democrats, labor unions soon gained power in Sweden. Most powerful was the labor unions' umbrella organization, the Swedish Trade Union Confederation (LO). Founded in 1898, LO now has more than two million members and may be the strongest labor organization in the world. Even today, Sweden remains one of the world's most unionized countries, with unions representing more than 80 percent of all workers.

As workers became organized, employers organized as well and formed a "union" of their own, the Swedish Employers' Confederation, in 1902. It was a shrewd move; during a general strike over national wage reduction in 1909, the workers had to give in to the employers, with a resulting loss of power.

From this rocky start, however, a level of cooperation developed between the two groups that enabled Sweden to avoid much of the labor unrest seen in other countries. Major strikes or lockouts were and are rare. All of the major players—trade unions, employers, the employers' union, government, and political parties—accepted the concepts of the welfare state in principle from the beginning, resulting in a high degree of consensus and mutual understanding. Admittedly, cooperation was made easier by the fact that more than half of Sweden's industry was owned by a handful of families who were ready and willing to forge alliances with the government.

In a historic 1938 meeting, labor and industry representatives agreed to rules for collective bargaining and a means to resolve labor disputes. This agreement, called the

"Saltsjöbads" agreement after the Stockholm suburb where it was signed, was unique because it was based not on law but on mutual understanding and benefit. The spirit of cooperation it engendered was subsequently referred to as the "Saltsjöbads" spirit.

The labor movement, which began as a result of poor living and working standards, was not unique to Sweden. The sense of injustice and indignation at the privilege of the upper classes was the basis for the emergence of communism. In Sweden there was a faction, primarily of young party members, who broke with the Social Democratic Party and founded the Communist Party (later the Left Party) as well. However, the more moderate views of the Social Democratic Party prevailed. As a result, the Social Democrats grew in strength, and by the time they won a major victory in 1932, they were able to begin a period of social reengineering, seeking a middle way between capitalism and communism: to create prosperity and security for all citizens, to battle unemployment, and to increase competitiveness, all without a revolution.

With the exception of a few months in 1936 and two short periods (1976–1982 and 1991–1994), the Social Democrats have remained in power, sometimes in a coalition, up to the present time.

Springboard to the Welfare State

Like most other countries, Sweden suffered during the Great Depression of the 1930s; more than one-third of its citizens were unemployed. Nevertheless, this period also served as a catalyst for change; the Social Democrats prepared numerous radical bills for social reform during these years. Unemployment benefits, launched in 1934, formed the foundation of the new welfare society. Although World War II slowed the reform, the Social Democrats passed comprehensive welfare legislation after the war that included pensions for the elderly, child allowances, housing allowances and subsidies, educational reform, and health insurance. The Social Democrats' pragmatic approach focused on finding solutions for the common good. Seeking and maintaining a balance between capitalism and a progressive and liberal social system were important components of the plan. Many of the reforms sought to create greater equality among the classes. One such reform instated a progressive taxation system that imposed high wealth taxes and high marginal taxes for high-wage earners to decrease the income gap and redistribute wealth from the very rich to the poor. The resulting revenues made the creation of a welfare system possible, one that presumably benefited everyone, not only those considered "needy." The society that resulted from these reforms has been given different labels: "the middle way," "the cradle-to-grave society," or simply, "the welfare state." The label matters little; what does matter is that every area of the Swedes' lives improved: housing, working conditions, child care, and health care.

The Values of Folkhemmet

Within Sweden, the new society became known as *folkhemmet*, or "the home of the people." Per Albin Hansson, one of the earliest Social Democratic prime ministers, first used this term in a political speech in the 1930s. Folkhemmet described how society, like the family, should take care of all its members and function with the welfare of each individual in mind.

The values underlying the Swedish Model are equality, fairness, a right to safety and security (*trygghet*), solidarity, the right to work, a social conscience, and environmental awareness. These egalitarian values are still embraced—and debated—today. Common themes on political posters and billboards during the country's 1999 elections included "fairness and justice for all," "care for everyone," and "no one should be treated differently." These themes contrast markedly with popular political messages in the United States, which tend to target the individual or special-interest groups, not society as a whole.

Equality

Perhaps most fundamental to the Swedish welfare system is the belief in equality. Although this subject is discussed at length in chapter 8, it is so central to Swedish society that we will mention it briefly here. Swedish social policy attempts to create a society without class, gender, or ethnic differences; this ideal was a key component in the development of the Swedish Model. In many ways equality has been attained. According to United Nations figures from 1998, Sweden is the most egalitarian country in the world; the poverty rate is less than 8 percent, about one-half that of the United States, Great Britain, or Germany. The situation is by no means perfect, however. Gender equality has come a long way, but disparities remain. Class differences are subtle, but they do exist, and as the income gap begins to increase, so may class differences. Perhaps most problematic is the question of ethnic and racial equality, which we will explore later. The fact is that much still needs to be done.

Fairness

Fairness is of prime importance in Sweden and can be very specifically defined: all should live well, but no one should have much more than anyone else does. In the United States, by way of contrast, fairness does not normally refer to what one has but to what opportunity one has. In his book *Hellre fattig än arbetslös?* (*Better Poor than Unemployed?*), Swedish author Per Wirtén points out that the types of low-paying service jobs that help reduce unemployment in the U.S. do not enable the working poor to enjoy a high standard of living. According to the Swedish definition of fairness, which is much narrower, this situation is not fair. In Swedish wage policies (which we will address in more detail in chapter 12), the differences among the wages of different professional groups as well as differences in actual wages among different job positions are much smaller than they are in the U.S.

Trygghet

Trygghet, or security and safety, is a critical goal of the Swedish Model. The welfare state acts as a safety net that allows Swedes to feel secure in their jobs, homes, and families. No one need fear homelessness or hunger; financial assistance, housing subsidies, training, and other forms of help are available through government agencies. This safety net enables individuals to develop a sense of independence and autonomy, their basic needs having been met.

Solidarity

Solidarity and working for the common good have long been guiding principles for the Swedish welfare system. Early on, Swedish farmers had to work together to survive. In the twentieth century, Swedes realized that as a small country, they had to work together if they wanted to interact successfully with the rest of the world. The Saltsjöbads agreement reinforced the value of all members of society coming together for mutual benefit.

Right to Work

To the Swedes, work is considered a basic right, seen as essential to maintaining one's sense of independence and self-sufficiency, which the Swedes value highly. Traditionally low unemployment in Sweden has fostered this belief over the years; work was virtually guaranteed. Labor laws that prohibited employers from firing anyone, except under extreme conditions, reinforced this belief. As a result, the high unemployment generated by the worldwide recession of the early 1990s came as a shock to the Swedes. Suddenly their basic right to work was no longer guaranteed, and for many, insecurity was hard, even frightening, to accept.

Social Conscience

In addition to focusing on national social reform, Sweden has taken an unusually strong interest, considering its size and location, in the welfare of the rest of the world, particularly that of underdeveloped countries. Because the Swedish Model values peace and nonviolence, human rights issues are considered important, no matter where they exist. In fact a feeling of responsibility toward groups denied their human rights played a major role in Sweden's immigration policies of the 1970s and 1980s, which allowed large numbers of political refugees to move to Sweden. The country also accepted many American conscientious objectors during the Vietnam War and criticized the United States openly for its involvement.

Environmental Awareness

Perhaps because of Sweden's vast expanses of wilderness and natural resources, the environment and its protection figure highly in people's consciousness. Most people recycle regularly. Laws regulate everything from food additives and chemical ingredients to the amount and kind of packaging material allowed. Children learn early to respect nature and tend to be very concerned about the environment as they grow up. The Green Party, with its focus on the environment, has enjoyed an upswing in popularity in recent years, and the environment is always on the political agenda.

Social and Economic Challenges

Sweden's most successful period under the Swedish Model spanned from 1945 to the early 1970s. Because of its policy of neutrality, Sweden escaped involvement in World War II and avoided its devastating consequences. The country subsequently leveraged its plentiful natural resources, which were desperately needed to reconstruct a war-torn Europe. Consequently, Sweden experienced remarkable economic growth during the postwar period.

During the course of a century, Sweden was transformed from a poor rural nation to a prosperous industrial nation with one of the highest standards of living in the world. Representatives from countries around the world came to witness the "miracle" and to take home ideas on how to balance entrepreneurial capitalism with social welfare. Over the last two decades, however, the Swedish Model has lost a bit of its former luster. During the recession of the early 1990s, per capita income declined, and unemployment reached its highest level in sixty years. A number of European countries have successfully adopted many of the most effective attributes of Sweden's social democracy and have achieved even better results; many have reached or surpassed Sweden's per capita income. Sweden's entry into the European Union (EU) in 1995 is likely to further erode remaining differences among the nations.

The Swedish welfare state now faces challenges that will test its very foundation. Two of the biggest are the changing face of the country's population and global economic factors.

The Impact of Immigration

During the development of the Swedish Model, Sweden was populated by people who had long shared a common history and culture. The immigration that began after World War II, when a larger workforce was needed, was limited, and most of the immigrants came from neighboring countries with similar cultures. Immigration patterns have changed, and the impact of large numbers of immigrants and refugees entering the country is testing the success of the Swedish Model.

Beginning in the early 1970s, increasing numbers of immigrants began coming to Sweden as part of a policy that opened up the country to political refugees. Since that time the portion of the population that can be classified as non-Swedish has increased dramatically. At the end of the twentieth century, first- and second-generation immigrants made up approximately 18 percent of the country's population. Sweden is no longer the linguistically and ethnically homogeneous culture it used to be; it is now a multilingual and multicultural society. This change has not come automatically. Although Swedes in general pride themselves on their tolerance, many have found these feelings tested when they have actually been confronted with immigrants with vastly different backgrounds. Ethnocentric, xenophobic behavior, so often criticized in other cultures, including the United States, has also surfaced in Sweden. Immigration has also placed heavy demands on the public sector, which in turn have strained the economy and, ultimately, the Swedes and their pocketbooks.

Swedes can be ambivalent when it comes to foreigners. Today, you will be hard-pressed to find a Swede who has not been abroad. Many show a tremendous interest in international cuisine, foreign languages, and all that is foreign. But traveling to distant lands and having brief encounters with people from other cultures is quite different from having someone with dramatically different values, beliefs, and behaviors living permanently next door. The Swedish Model was built, quite frankly, with Swedish values in mind.

During the 1980s and 1990s, Sweden saw a marked increase in crime, much of which was rightly or wrongly attributed to immigrants. Although the great majority of immigrants are law-abiding, some have undoubtedly taken advantage of the social system; others, unemployed and trapped in segregated neighborhoods or refugee communities, may have resorted to crime because of an inability to assimilate into Swedish society. Crime among immigrants has understandably not eased the distrust of the Swedes toward many of the immigrant groups with their many different customs and belief systems.

Immigrants face their own troubles. Unemployment is much higher among them than among Swedes in general. They are often underemployed because their educational or professional credentials are not accepted in Sweden; they are often stuck in jobs with poorer working conditions. Moreover, the number of ethnic enclaves with lower-than-average living conditions seems to be growing. Many studies also show that the children of immigrants are not adapting well, as seen in physical symptoms as well as high suicide rates among teenagers with immigrant backgrounds.

The Swedish government provides immigrants with significant financial assistance, but many Swedes argue that the lack of gainful employment and consequent inability to be self-sufficient (a core Swedish value) make it difficult for newcomers to become truly integrated into society.

The situation is not all bleak, however. Immigration has changed Sweden in many positive ways as well. The new multicultural society has created a greater openness and has stimulated creativity. Sweden has become a much more global and colorful place to live for everyone.

Economic Stressors

In addition to the changes brought about by Sweden's increasingly diverse population, global economic factors have also challenged the Swedish Model.

The energy crisis of the 1970s severely affected Sweden, decreasing industrial production for the first time in many years. The drop in production was especially alarming because it had been the engine behind Sweden's growth into a welfare state.

During the same time period, increased competition from foreign countries where low wages were the norm strained shipbuilding, shoe manufacturing, and textiles industries, among others, causing some industries to close their doors permanently. Exacerbating the situation were extreme local wage hikes, which increased wages by 40 percent as a result of collective bargaining.

At the same time, the welfare state's entitlements and benefits grew to what can in retrospect be seen as an excessive degree. It became clear that implementing all the new reforms was going to be too expensive. The population was aging and the need for elder care increasing. It also became apparent that some social benefits were being abused in a manner that had not been predicted. Finally, the country had to assume the high cost involved in taking care of the widening stream of political refugees.

Before the 1970s there had been little discord between industry and the labor unions. By the beginning of the 1970s, however, this began to change. New labor laws were enacted, resulting in more power for the workers and their unions. They began to have a significant voice in bargaining with the corporations, and their demands increased. In addition, laws were passed that prohibited the firing of employees, even with cause. All this had an adverse effect on the spirit of cooperation between labor and management. As a result, although the unions are still strong, discontent has risen rapidly, especially among employers, who face increasing pressure to compete globally.

Moving Forward

In many ways one might see the so-called glory days of the Swedish Model as a Pollyanna existence for Sweden. It had achieved a very orderly society, with plenty for all and almost nonexistent poverty. Taxes were high, but there was very little crime. Good schools and a social safety net gave inhabitants a sense of security unknown in most parts of the world. Perhaps, as the quote at the beginning of this chapter expressed, the Swedish Model was indeed a success only because a specific time in history and a certain set of demographics made it possible to create a society that was able for a time to combine the best of social and business interests. But as you will see in the rest of this book, the Swedes continue to be proud of how far they have come and how much they have influenced other nations.

3

The Four S's: Sex, Suicide, Socialism, and Spirits

Everybody knows that the Swedes, after leading a dull and yet (paradoxically) eventful life divided between free sex and rigid socialism, all end up (understandably) committing suicide. Everybody knows this but the Swedes.
—Dr. Göran Sonesson, Lund University

Summary: Over the past fifty years, three things have come to mind when Sweden is mentioned: sex, suicide, and socialism. These stereotypes, along with that of the perpetually drunken Swede, may have some foundation in fact but are much exaggerated. Swedes are not sex-crazed, but they are less concerned with public nudity, and relations between the sexes are more egalitarian. Some Swedes do commit suicide, of course, but the country's streak of cultural melancholy and a preoccupation with statistics may have inflated this morbid reputation. Socialism is not the same as social democracy, the political system that created Sweden's welfare state. And although Swedes have historically been a hard-drinking people, they are also subject to the highest alcohol taxes and strictest regulations in the world.

Blame it on Ike. America's (if not the world's) modern image of Sweden may have originated from remarks made by Dwight D. Eisenhower at a Republican Party convention meeting in Chicago in July 1960. He referred to an unnamed European nation whose "socialistic philosophy" had caused its suicide rate to rise "almost unbelievably" and where "drunkenness" and "lack of ambition" were pervasive.

Add sex, and you have Sweden's "Four S's," which have dominated the international view of the country for nearly half a century. Like most stereotypes, these, too, have some roots in reality. Nonetheless, the facts are much less compelling than the myths.

"There has never been any particularly impressive amount of suicide, sex or socialism in Sweden," wrote Göran Sonesson, Ph.D., an associate professor of cultural semiotics at Lund University. This is proven, he said, "in the first instance, by statistics (and there are a lot of statistics in Sweden), and in the two other instances...mainly [by the experience] of disappointed foreigners in one case, and that of disappointed Swedes in the other" (Sonesson 1995, 12).

In fact, many Swedes find the stereotypes represented by the Four S's tiresome, and some even find them offensive.

Sex

The Myth: Swedes are sexually preoccupied and promiscuous.

The Facts: Sex and Sweden have long been linked in the minds of many foreigners. Swedish women in particular have been admired not only for their stereotypical blonde good looks, but equally for a perceived sexual availability.

This reputation is due in large part to the Swedes' open attitude about sex and nudity, but it is an attitude that has been exaggerated in many cases by movies. Progressive films by Swedish director Ingmar Bergman in the 1950s and a small number of sexually explicit films in the 1960s—*I Am Curious*

(*Yellow*) directed by Vilgot Sjöman is the classic example—led to Sweden's reputation as a sexually liberal society. Today, the word *Schwedenfilm* (Sweden film) means "pornographic film" in German. And in the United States, the word *Swedish* is sometimes applied as an adjective to increase the sex appeal of products from beer (as in one American beer company's TV commercials featuring the "Swedish Bikini Team") to otherwise ordinary massage oils or condoms. Anyone coming to Sweden expecting to encounter sexual abandon, however, has been misled. The Swedes, young and old, are no more promiscuous or sexually outrageous than people in other Western European countries. In truth they may even seem rather prudish in comparison. The difference lies in the frank way in which they approach and discuss sexuality (Rekdal 1997).

As in other areas of their lives, Swedes tend to be rational and practical when it comes to sexual matters. They discuss sex openly without self-consciousness or the shame or guilt frequently associated with religious beliefs in other countries. Sweden is a rather secularized society that views sex not as something "bad" or sinful but as natural and normal and something that logically requires planning.

For example, teenagers have easy access to contraception; the rationale: young people are likely to be sexually adventurous, and trying to enforce abstinence is impractical. Instead, Swedes promote sex education and the prevention of unplanned pregnancies and sexually transmitted diseases. Family-planning services and contraception advice are available to people of all ages, based on the principle that women must be allowed to decide the number and spacing of children they wish to have (The Swedish Institute 2000a).

Sweden was among the earliest nations to take up family planning. In 1933 Elise Ottosen-Jensen, a Norwegian planned-parenthood pioneer married to a Swede, founded the National Organization for Sexual Information (RFSU), an organization that is still active in Sweden. Today, RFSU and similar organizations offer counseling and information on sexual issues to anyone and actively promote AIDS education and awareness.

As a result of easy access to education and contraception and a realistic attitude toward sex, Sweden's teen pregnancy rate is much lower than that of the United States. Sweden currently has one of the lowest birthrates in Europe. At 1.5 children per Swedish female (The Swedish Institute 1997), the rate is so low that deaths in Sweden outpaced births in 1997; immigration, however, compensated for the population shortfall.

Sweden first permitted abortion in 1938, but for medical and some humanitarian reasons only; restrictions on abortions were lifted in 1975. Abortion may be performed until the eighteenth week of pregnancy on request and at minimal cost. Although antiabortion groups exist in Sweden, they do not have the political clout that such groups have in the United States.

The distinction between sex and nudity is also important in addressing the stereotype; in Sweden nudity does not automatically equal sex. Children often play unclothed on the beach until they are six or seven years old. Women of all ages and body types sunbathe topless by the pool or at the beach during Sweden's short summer. To misinterpret this activity as sexual availability, however, is seen as ignorant and insulting. Nor is nudity censored on television and in films as it is in the United States; the Swedes are much more concerned about depicting images of violence. It is not shocking to see an ad or photograph of a nude man or woman in the daily or weekly press. To most Swedes nudity outside of a sexual context just isn't a big deal.

This does not mean that pornography doesn't exist in Sweden, of course, but that Swedes have been fairly tolerant of it, within limits. Many Swedes were caught off-guard by a report of hard-core pornography being produced in Sweden and aired on late-night cable TV, easily accessible to children and adolescents.

Shocking Truth, a quasi-documentary film by Swedish film-maker Alexa Wolf, ignited a debate on the potential dangers of pornography. The film, which aired on Swedish TV in early 2000, suggested a connection between hard pornography and increased sexual aggression (including reported group rapes) among teenage boys. Critics insisted that no connection had been substantiated, but the Swedish Parliament saw a wave of speakers on the subject after the film aired.

Swedish sexual mores are also clashing with those of the country's numerous immigrants, many of whom originate from Muslim cultures. In a series of interviews, Swedish newspapers during the debate reported that young Middle Eastern men and teenagers had been targeting Swedish women for rape, asserting that raping a Swedish woman was not as bad as raping one from their own countries. A Swedish woman, they rationalized, had likely "already had lots of men" and had no family honor at stake. The interviews raised concern among people in Sweden from all cultural backgrounds.

Social attitudes have also changed regarding relationships. During the last thirty years, an increasing number of couples have been choosing to live together without getting married. Compared with many other countries, this practice has gained acceptance fairly quickly in Sweden. If you are introduced to someone's *sambo* (literally, "living together"), you have met a significant other who is a live-in partner but not a spouse. Couples in long-term relationships who choose to live apart may even sometimes refer to each other as their *särbo* ("living apart") to stress the difference.

Many of these couples have children who may participate in their parents' wedding—if and when their parents decide to get married. Some practical folks even choose to have their child baptized at the same time. To conservative-minded Americans this may seem very untraditional, to say the least, but in Sweden these practices and family units are both common and accepted.

Suicide

The Myth: Swedes kill themselves in greater numbers than most people.

The Facts: People do commit suicide in Sweden, as they do the world over. The incidence of suicide in Sweden compared with other countries, however, is inflated by the stereotype. In comparing suicide rates, the presence and accuracy of statistics are important. Many countries whose religious or societal beliefs consider taking one's own life a mortal sin or a crime may choose not to keep official statistics on the subject; not so in Sweden, home to *Statistiska Centralbyrån* (SCB), Statistics Sweden. The fact is, the Swedes are probably world specialists at statistics (Phillips-Martinsson 1991). Suicide has been included in Swedish population statistics (starting in church records) since the 1600s, and this may contribute to the country's prominent reputation concerning *självmord*—literally, "self-murder."

Even among countries that do track suicide rates, Sweden ranks far from the top. Statistics compiled by the World Health Organization in Geneva show that Sweden, with an annual suicide rate of 14.2 people per 100,000, actually ranks lower than many of its European neighbors. Hungary (32.9) and the Baltic nations of Finland (24.7), Estonia (34.9), Latvia (36.0), and Lithuania (43.7) report some of the highest suicide rates in the world. Sweden's suicide rate is slightly higher than that of the United States (11.5) and Canada (12.3). Recent figures indicate that approximately 20,000 people attempt to commit suicide in Sweden every year; 1,200 of them tragically succeeded in 1997.

*Table: Reported Annual Suicide Rates of Selected Countries**

Country	Year (most recent year available as of October 2000)	Suicide Rate (per 100,000)
Canada	1997	12.3
Denmark	1996	17.0
Estonia	1998	34.9
Finland	1996	24.7
France	1997	19.2
Germany	1998	14.4
Hungary	1998	32.9
Latvia	1998	36.0
Lithuania	1998	43.7
Netherlands	1996	10.1
Norway	1995	12.6
Russian Federation	1997	39.3
Sweden	**1996**	**14.2**
United Kingdom	1997	7.1
United States	1997	11.5

If these are the facts, then what is the origin of the stereotype? Some point to Sweden's pre-Christian past, the Viking era, when a useless mouth to feed was a burden. The elderly sometimes took their own lives when they could work no more. There was no moral stigma attached to suicide; instead, it was a sign of courage (Elstob 1979).

---

* The source for these statistics is the World Heath Organization, Geneva, 2000. Some countries have been omitted for space considerations.

In fact suicide was not punishable by law in Sweden until the Middle Ages with the rise of Christianity and the Augustinian doctrine, which decreed suicide sinful. This view was intensified by the Protestant Reformation, which used the Bible as an authority in both crimes and their punishment. The bodies of suicides were subjected to degradation and were not buried in cemeteries. Individuals who attempted suicide were whipped or imprisoned. Suicide was eventually decriminalized in 1864. Subsequently, even those assisting in or instigating suicide have been free from punishment if their actions do not constitute manslaughter.

Others trace the suicidal stereotype to long, dark winters and the "Ingmar Bergman syndrome"—referring to the filmmaker's often dark cinematic vision that suggests the angst or melancholy that is often posited as a prominent Swedish national characteristic. Northern Swedish winters are, indeed, long and dark. Furthermore, as will be discussed in the next chapter, there is a fondness in traditional Swedish folk culture for the contemplation of things past, for the bittersweet and the longing reminiscences featured in the melancholic tunes of the country's national poets, writers, and composers.

Also, Swedes are often reluctant to express strong emotions, including anger or disapproval, a theme that emerges in many areas of Swedish culture. An American psychologist once noted that among his Swedish suicide cases it was "particularly difficult for them...to give open expression of anger, or a frank criticism of anyone in their immediate surroundings" (Austin 1968, 33).

A 1970 report found that problems on the job and in one's finances entered into the picture in at least one-half of the Swedish suicides investigated. A more recent study by the Institute for Social Research at Stockholm University (1996) found that about 10 percent of all suicides are related to unemployment. As we have already mentioned, the Swedes have a long tradition of not wishing to be a burden on others.

And as we will take up later, in chapter 5, carrying one's weight (working, in other words) is very important. The same 1996 study found that between 30 and 40 percent of all suicide attempts by men stem from alcohol abuse. The explanation given was that alcohol abuse leads to isolation and depression, conditions that are commonly related to suicide in general.

Sweden's suicide statistics remain relatively static and lower than foreigners assume. The only population group that has seen a marked increase in suicides in recent years is teenagers of immigrant families—a sad reflection of their difficulty in adjusting culturally, socially, and personally to life in Sweden.

Socialism

The Myth: Sweden is one of the last bastions of socialism.

The Facts: Is Sweden really a socialist country? The answer depends on how you define the term *socialism*. If you ask the average Swede, however, he or she will likely emphasize that Sweden is foremost a democracy that offers its citizens many social benefits—a social welfare state and thus a social democracy.

Sweden is also a capitalist country, which makes it somewhat of a paradox. It has the world's strongest trade unions, yet it has spawned many well-known multinational corporations, such as Ericsson, ABB, Electrolux, Volvo, and Saab. Although Sweden's labor party, the Social Democrats, has been in power for most of the past seventy years, state ownership of business has ranked lower than in many industrialized countries; in 1997 the state owned less than 10 percent of businesses compared with over 30 percent in France (Rekdal 1997).

In any case the Swedish concept of socialism does not have the negative connotations it has for Americans. To many Americans, socialism is nearly synonymous with communism, a reviled form of government. Many also associate it with socialized medicine, a health-care delivery system that few Americans understand and that U.S. politicians have denounced as "un-American."

To Swedes, however, socialism refers to caring for society as a whole and extending social welfare to all. Compared with the United States, where the individual's rights tend to come first, Sweden places more emphasis on the benefit to the group than on the benefit to the individual. This focus has been reinforced over the decades since the Social Democratic Party came to power in 1932. Many Swedes see the rapid rise of their country from one that was very poor to one that has among the highest standards of living in the world as a direct result of the Social Democratic government.

As discussed in chapter 2, the sociopolitical model that developed, folkhemmet, was designed to provide security and well-being for all citizens. Despite the problematic changes that occurred during the early 1990s, such as high unemployment and cuts in social benefits, support for the Social Democratic Party remains strong. Swedes feel a great sense of pride over what they perceive to be an evolved and mature society, one where there has been little room for anything considered out of the norm.

One reason that Swedes have embraced this very structured system to such a degree is "the conviction that 'collective' decision making—that is, decision making by central authorities—guarantees the greatest justice" (Daun 1996, 138). Traditionally, the central government has enjoyed a high degree of acceptance that contrasts sharply with that of many other countries, especially the United States, where a distrust of government is almost a part of the national character. The 1990s, however, saw some of that acceptance and trust erode in Sweden—a process that, according to political scientist Tommy Möller of Stockholm University, had been under way since the 1970s.

In the early 1990s a nonsocialist coalition government was elected and began to make some major changes, including cutting certain subsidies. But it went too far too fast by Swedish standards, and by the next election, the Social Democratic Party was once again in control. As the expression goes, "better the devil you know." The Social Democrats continued some of the cutbacks but also tried to retain many of the support systems in line with the philosophy of "the people's home."

Spirits

The Myth: Swedes are world-leading consumers of alcohol, particularly hard liquor, or "spirits."

The Facts: In 1467 a Stockholm merchant received a shipment of "aqua vitae," an alcoholic elixir used to produce gunpowder; it was soon discovered that one could also drink the liquid. "Aquavit," as it is now called, had found a permanent home in Sweden.

The Swedes have historically had an ambivalent relationship with alcohol, struggling with the question of social alcohol policy for more than one hundred years. Despite its liberal, free-living image, the country has traditionally had one of the most restrictive alcohol policies in Europe. It also has some of the toughest laws in the world against drunk driving: a blood-alcohol limit of 0.02—a virtually zero-tolerance policy.

Sweden is nestled in the so-called "vodka belt" with other northern European countries such as Finland, Russia, and Poland; and like their neighbors, the Swedes have historically preferred spirits such as vodka over beer and wine, the beverages of choice for nations further south (Phillips-Martinsson 1991). In the early 1900s it was not unusual for employers to give blue-collar workers a *snaps* on the job to keep them warm and motivated. At that time Swedes consumed ten gallons of alcoholic beverages, largely aquavit and *brännvin* (a spiced aquavit often distilled at home), per capita each year (Childs 1947). This high rate of consumption has been blamed on the country's long, cold, dark winters as well as on the Swedes' tendency for melancholy—yet another stubborn stereotype.

As in other cultures, alcohol acts as a social lubricant for Swedes. One of the social and psychological functions of drinking in Swedish culture, writes ethnologist Åke Daun, is "to lessen the individual's fear of making a fool of him- or herself—for example, the anxiety people feel about saying the wrong thing" (1996, 51). Alcohol helps some Swedes relax, assume a different "identity," and feel less inhibited. As in Japan, another culture where rigid social conformity exists, something done while intoxicated "doesn't count." Unfortunately, this has led to an unflattering image abroad; some Swedes on vacation in countries far from home overindulge and have been known to make fools of themselves.

The Swedish government, concerned about the health risks of alcohol consumption, stepped in during the early 1900s to implement strict controls. Public rationing, enforced through monthly quota books, continued until 1955. While American public service announcements urge citizens to drink responsibly, the Swedish government's unabashed goal continues to be to control its people's alcohol consumption.

For many years Sweden strictly limited the amount of alcohol individuals could import, and it continues to monopolize domestic sales through a chain of state-owned stores called *Systembolaget* (Systemet). Unlike in other European countries, not even wine or beer (except for low- or nonalcoholic types) can be purchased at the local grocery store. For Swedes, waiting an hour in the queue at the local Systemet to buy a nice bottle of wine or a six-pack of beer on Friday evening—even longer the day before a major holiday—is an unavoidable part of life. Yet, some people are embarrassed; no one is fooled by the subtly patterned plastic bag disguising the alcohol within, and many a Swede has tucked that bag into a sack or briefcase to hide it from prying eyes or ears. Even the sound of clinking bottles carries a stigma for some people.[†]

Through pricing and selection Systemet encourages the consumption of wine and beer over hard liquor. The taxes levied on alcoholic beverages in Sweden—the highest in Europe—would make a U.S. Republican blanch. Nearly 90 percent of the price of a bottle of Swedish brännvin is tax (the more liberal EU import limits could drastically cut the state's income). Sweden tries to justify its policies by advertising the health benefits of teetotaling in its stores.

Based on reported alcohol sales, the Swedish government asserts that its efforts have worked. Sweden ranked last among EU countries in terms of total alcohol sales in Europe in 1998, at 4.9 liters per inhabitant. This is substantially less than the 13.3 liters purchased annually by the Luxembourgers, who lead the list (Systembolaget 2000). Swedes reportedly suffer fewer alcohol-related illnesses as well.

As a result of the high prices at home, Swedes traveling abroad have traditionally stocked up on alcohol for the return trip, although for many years, if caught bringing in more than one liter of spirits or two liters of wine per person, they could be slapped with a misdemeanor charge under Swedish law. That policy has changed, though, as Sweden gradually loosens its restrictions to come into line with guidelines set by the European Union. The EU allows individuals to bring home up to ten liters of spirits and 90 liters of wine per person.

Sweden didn't surrender to EU regulations without a fight, however. In 1996 the EU Court ruled that the nation could

---

[†] Why would a Swede be embarrassed to have someone know he or she had bought a drink? "The Americans' cognitive dissonance about sexual matters is almost identical to that of the Swedes and alcohol," suggested Marc Bünger, an American management consultant who lived in Sweden for five years. "It is a question of what you do in public versus what you do behind closed doors" (2000).

retain Systemet and its alcohol monopoly through retail outlets. Sweden was also allowed to keep in place its import restrictions under an exemption to EU rules granted when Sweden joined in 1995. Sweden sought a five-year extension to the exemption, which expired in June 2000, on health grounds: Swedish officials produced a report from the Public Health Institute that estimated the number of alcohol-related deaths would rise by one thousand per year if the spirit policies of the EU applied to Sweden. But European regulators had little sympathy.

Some pundits predict that Systemet won't survive if restrictions are relaxed. So much cheaper European liquor is already flowing in through the country's borders that Systemet is losing money in some areas. Systemet has reacted by taking steps to become more customer-friendly. In 2000, it started a trial opening of about one-third of its 397 shops on Saturday—the first time in eighteen years that Swedes were able to buy alcohol on the weekend. (Systemets were open on Saturdays until 1982, when a four-month trial of dry Saturdays found the number of house break-ins fell by 7 percent and assaults by 8 percent.) At one suburban Stockholm outlet, customers standing in an endlessly long Friday-night line were treated to live entertainment while they waited.

"For Americans, this might not sound like much, but I assure you, if you tell a Swede who has not been home in a few years, his jaw will drop to his knees," wrote Swedish author and columnist Ulf Nilson (1998, 7).

4

National Pride: A Matter of Romance

Jag är så glad att jag är svensk!
(I am so happy I am Swedish!)
—Swedish popular song lyric

Summary: Swedish national pride bears little resemblance to the nationalism seen in other European countries. Instead, it can be viewed more as a national romance; Swedes are in love with an idealized picture of their country and how life should be. They are proud of their sociopolitical system, their down-to-earth monarchy, and their country's engineering tradition. They love the works of their folk poets and musicians; they crave the melancholy celebration of Sweden's natural beauty and cultural heritage; they are sentimental about the Swedish flag, more an item of decoration than a symbol of chauvinism. Although the Swedes' national romance persists today, the country's idealized vision of itself took a hard blow with the assassination of Prime Minister Olof Palme in 1986. In addition a more political form of nationalism has emerged since Sweden joined the European Union in 1995.

Most Swedes are proud of their national heritage. They take pride in their country's system of social equality and those who pioneered it. They are proud of Sweden's inventors and engineers; its artists, musicians, and athletes; and its political nonalignment, not to mention its reputation abroad for high-quality products and innovative, modern designs. They are pleased when people abroad acknowledge their country's accomplishments and recognize well-known Swedes—or anyone with a connection to Sweden.

"If there is an American athlete with a remote Swedish ancestor, then he or she instantly becomes a 'step-Swede,'" joked an American living in Sweden.

Even among Swedes who leave Sweden, most tend to hang on to their Swedishness after many years abroad—in some cases embracing traditional customs and behaving more "Swedish" than they ever did at home.

But Swedish national pride bears little resemblance to the nationalism that has emerged in Europe over the last few decades. Although Sweden shares many cultural traits with its neighbors, it has no independence day or liberation to celebrate, unlike Norway, which commemorates its independence from Danish rule in 1814 on May 17 and its liberation from the Nazi occupation of World War II in 1945 on May 8. In addition, although Swedes are loyal and devoted to their country, they do not attempt to impose their culture on other nations, nor does their national pride resemble the patriotism of the Stars and Stripes variety.

Instead, the Swedes' relationship to their country is more a national romance: the affection of a happy, yet strangely melancholy, people for an idealized, peaceful society where the season is always summer. The fact that this Swedish idyll—like the perfect Christmas—never truly existed in reality is unimportant. What matters is that it could.

The Model Society

Sweden's pride covers many areas of Swedish life: the sociopolitical ideal, the down-to-earth monarchy, the country's engineering tradition. Then there is the cultural-emotional *nationalromantik* attached to the country's folk poets and musicians and their evocation of the feelings Swedes have for their heritage, including the Swedish flag, a symbol more of decoration than of chauvinism.

As we have discussed, the Swedes stand behind folkhemmet and what it represents: equality, fairness, justice, a right to safety and security, and solidarity. Many Swedes grew up at a time when Sweden was seen as a modern ideal in many ways—a country that had leveled the playing field for its citizens and alleviated much of the poverty and misery found in other countries (including parts of the United States). The Swedes take pride in a system that they perceive as more evolved, humane, and mature than those in which people have to compete for survival or live to attain wealth.

Of course, the Swedes have their own way of expressing pride. Swedish modesty, as we'll discuss in more detail in chapter 6 on the *lagom* phenomenon, frowns on anything that seems like boasting—even when it is patriotic and not personal.

"Is there anything typically Swedish?" the Stockholm daily newspaper *Svenska Dagbladet* asked rhetorically. "Maybe it's not letting on that you're proud to be Swedish." And if you do, you do so only with reservations. When Social Democrat Ingvar Carlsson ran for reelection as prime minister in 1994, he described the feelings he had as a young man visiting Chicago for the first time. Surrounded by such poverty in the richest country in the world, "I was almost proud to live in a country like Sweden," he said (Palmer 2000, 104). Would an American president who said he was "almost" proud to be an American be reelected? Run out of town on a rail is more likely.

Still, there is an assumption, spoken or unspoken, that every country would be like Sweden if it could. An American woman working in Sweden in the early 1990s became aware of this form of pride when a Swedish friend pointed out that "the 'new' countries in Eastern Europe are looking at Sweden as a model for their governments."

Although the relationship between industry and labor is no longer as harmonious as it once was, Sweden remains one of the world's most unionized countries. Swedes are proud of their country's history of solving labor problems rationally, avoiding the national strikes and other labor unrest other nations have not.

At one time the Swedes were quite proud of their military history, the glory years of the 1600s, when Sweden was a great power in Europe, but after the nation's defeat by Russia in the early nineteenth century, after which it surrendered Finland, the focus of its pride shifted. With its defeats, Sweden embarked, as we mentioned earlier, on a path of neutrality in peacetime and nonalignment in war. (This did not, however, prevent its sympathies in World War I from being divided and those in World War II from leaning strongly toward the Allies.) Pacifism became increasingly valued. Today, Swedes are as proud of their pacifism and neutrality, based on a belief in nonviolent solutions to problems, as people in other nations are of their military muscle.

Pointing to its own nonalignment as a model, Sweden was particularly critical of U.S. involvement in the Vietnam War; the country took in many American conscientious objectors. Today, Swedes (and Scandinavians in general) are proud of the role the Scandinavian countries have played in hosting peace talks among players in the Middle East and in leading UN peacekeeping efforts.

As a result, it is not uncommon for Swedes to judge other countries using their own experience and standards and to find other countries lacking. Some might call this attitude nationalistic; non-Swedes living in the country tend to shrug their shoulders and simply call it arrogant or naïve.

Pride in the Monarchy

It may seem somewhat odd that an egalitarian country like Sweden has a monarchy with a king, royal family, and royal palace. In some of the other remaining monarchies of the world, kings and queens still wield varying degrees of power, but in Sweden, the role of King Carl XVI Gustav is strictly ceremonial. Over the years Swedes have periodically discussed abolishing the monarchy, but most people seem to support it, particularly the older generations. In fact Sweden's royal family is quite popular. The monarchy received a real boost when the king married the German-Brazilian commoner Silvia Sommerlath in the 1970s. A charming and intelligent woman, she has delighted the Swedish people and is often named along with author Astrid Lindgren (creator of Pippi Longstocking, among other memorable characters) as one of the most admired women in Sweden. Her daughter, Crown Princess Victoria, is not far behind. The royal family also includes Prince Carl Philip and Princess Madeleine.

Swedes are proud of the dignified, modest way in which their monarchs behave. Their lives are followed with great interest in the Swedish press but so far have provided far less fodder for the paparazzi than, for example, the British royals. One reason Swedish royal family members have remained so popular is because they live a fairly normal life without much excess and extravagance. As we will discuss in coming chapters, the egalitarian Swedes would never put up with monarchs who truly thought themselves to be better than anyone else.

Quality and Technology

In a society of equals, there is little room for heroes. Interestingly, some of those who come closest to holding that position in Sweden are the great inventors and scholars the country has produced. If you haven't heard of them, ask any Swede; he or she will be happy to inform you.

For a country of its size, Sweden has produced an impressive number of inventions. This is due, in part, to the importance that Sweden has always placed on engineering, an emphasis that some trace back to the innovative builders of the Viking ships. The Swedes point to Swedish-American John Ericsson, who built the iron-clad *Monitor* for the Union forces during the American Civil War, as an heir to this tradition.

Near the end of the nineteenth century, several companies produced innovations that led to their becoming multinational giants. These companies are frequently referred to in Sweden as the "genius firms" and include Volvo, Electrolux, and Ericsson.

Lars Magnus Ericsson, a former farmer, blacksmith, and railroad worker, received a scholarship to study electrotechnology in 1876. He began working on telegraphs, but after learning of Alexander Graham Bell's telephone, he decided to make telephones. In addition to developing a desk telephone with a hand-held microphone, Ericsson developed equipment for entire telephone networks. By the mid-1880s, he had produced the first automatic telephone switchboards. In 1903, when Ericsson retired from management, his company was already a global operation. Today, Ericsson employs nearly 100,000 people worldwide and is a major player in the global telecommunications industry.

Another of the country's famous inventors is Alfred Nobel, who created dynamite. Today, his name is most frequently connected with the Nobel Prizes that were established, at his request, through a foundation after his death. Other lesser-known Swedish innovations include the following:

- *the safety match.* In 1844 Gustaf Erik Pasch created an alternative to commonly used matches that contained poisonous white phosphorus. The safety match did not become a success, however, until a Swedish mechanic named Alexander Lagerman built a machine that made it possible to manufacture safety matches cost-effectively, which led to mass production. Today, more than one hundred countries import the Swedish safety match.

- *the modern zipper.* An American by the name of Whitcomb Jones had already obtained a patent for a device called a "zip" as early as 1893. The problem was that it didn't work. Swede Gideon Sundbäck came up with a new design in 1913 that looked much like the zippers of today; he is therefore credited as its inventor.

- *the steel ball bearing.* In 1905 Sven Winquist, a young engineer, encountered problems operating certain machinery at the textile factory where he worked. The solution to the problem was the ball bearing. To produce this product, Winquist founded a company called Svenska Kullagerfabriken (SKF). By 1918 the company had twelve thousand employees in several countries.

Famous Swedish scholars include scientist, botanist, and physician Carl von Linné, who developed the system of binomial nomenclature with which he classified plants and animals. This system, which gives every creature a genus name and species name (e.g., *Homo sapiens*), appeared in the publication *Systema Naturae* in 1735. The Celsius temperature scale was developed by and named for Anders Celsius, an astronomer and mathematician at the University of Uppsala, Sweden's oldest university.

Sweden and quality became synonymous during the twentieth century, as well-made Swedish products found their way into the global marketplace. Quality, of course, is a concept that often depends on the eye of the beholder. In Sweden quality implies something that is well designed, that always works, and that lasts a long time. Ask a Swede still driving a 1981 Volvo what he or she thinks about the American penchant for trading in cars every three years—the answer is, not much. Swedes in the United States often complain about the lack of care and craftsmanship they see in homes, cars, and household items. They criticize "disposable" products, and "buy quality; cry once" is their motto.

This position, however, does not always work to their advantage. In fact from a business perspective, it can sometimes pose problems. For example, Swedish companies often decide to tackle the U.S. market with the belief that the high quality of their products will sell itself. In the United States, however, many other aspects are factored into sales, including price, accessibility, and image—all of which must be communicated through marketing. Swedish pride can obstruct marketing; the Swedes resent having to explain why their product is the best. Isn't it obvious? It's Swedish!

The Swedish Nationalromantik

It is difficult at times to believe a country of rational engineers could turn out to be romantics at heart, but romantic they are. The Swedish nationalromantik can be experienced through the country's rich tradition of folk songs and verse. Sweden is a country of moods, the essence of which is captured in its melodic poems, which are characterized by a fondness for the melancholy, for the celebration of nature, for the outdoor life, and for the common man.

Even the Swedish national anthem, "Du gamla du fria" ("You Ancient, You Free [Land]") is an ode to nature. The song makes a brief reference to Sweden's past glory days as a European power, but it focuses primarily on the country's beauty. "Thy sun, thy skies, thy verdant meadows smiling" move the Swede just as "bombs bursting in air" to illuminate a flag might move someone from another nation.

Among Europeans the Swedes (and perhaps the Finns or Norwegians) rival only the Portuguese in embracing the melancholic. But while the Portuguese saldage captures the emotions of longing for the distant lover, the Swedish vemod expresses a nation's collective remembrance of an idealized past—a time of toil and struggle but also of natural beauty and harmony.

"The Swedish gift...is for a certain elegiac melancholy, derived, perhaps, from a vivid sense of the unattainability of an ardently desired perfection" (Austin 1968, 128). For all their pride in their "ideal," modern society, "the Swedes also feel a real need to brood, reminisce, and drink *brännvin*," explained one Swede. Life is hard, but oh, so beautiful. And this isn't just a psychological result of long, dark winters, as non-Swedes assume. Swedes are moved by the pathos of poetry and song describing the solitude of the forests, the existence of the working man, and the fundamental subjects of life and death. These songs represent the romantic side of the Swedes, the passion hidden beneath their reserved and rational behavior.

Few of Sweden's folk poets and musicians capture vemod as well as Dan Andersson (1888–1920), a man of working-class background who was recognized posthumously as one of the country's foremost poets and novelists. His works, many of which have been set to music, describe the life of working-class Finnmark, the rural central Swedish region of his birth. Andersson was a man whose life was dominated by work and punctuated by happiness, sadness, and death. He lived his entire life in extreme poverty, taking many different jobs, including that of the charcoal burner—a lonely, dirty job that he later depicted in several poems. Andersson achieved little recognition for his writing during his lifetime, but a cult developed around his work after his death, and his body of work is still admired today.*

On a brilliant summer day, however, it is not the bittersweet poems of Andersson that are sung, but more likely the lyrical ballads of Evert Taube (1890–1976) or the lusty verses of Carl-Michael Bellman (1740–1795).

---

* Befitting his tragic life, he died young and needlessly of cyanide poisoning in a hotel room in Stockholm in 1920. Cyanide was commonly used to kill fleas and other pests, and the bedding in his room had been aired badly.

Taube holds a unique place in both Swedish music and Swedish hearts. Perhaps the most beloved Swedish troubadour of modern times, he was equally an author, singer, composer, and artist. He was a prolific writer and composer, with more than two hundred songs to his name. It wasn't until later in life that he was taken seriously by critics as an author and poet. He often illustrated his own books as well.

A sailor in his youth, Taube wrote widely on his voyages in the southern oceans, with many songs set in South America, where he lived for five years. His songs depicted the colorful sailor's life and the beauty of the archipelago of Roslagen, north of Stockholm, and of Sweden's rugged western coast in Bohuslän. He wrote everything from lusty ballads about the bars and bordellos of his travels to exquisitely beautiful love songs. His songs have been translated into and performed in many languages; there is hardly a Swede alive who doesn't know several of them by heart. For those who don't, the host of any good Swedish summer party provides a homemade, photocopied songbook for group singing during the festivities (only the words are included; everyone, it is assumed, knows the famous melodies). Among the best known are "Calle Schewen's Waltz," an ode to Roslagen, "The Letter from Lillan," and "The Beautiful Helén" (or, "The Girl in Peru").

Bellman predates Andersson and Taube by more than one hundred years, but his pastoral compositions and spirited depictions of life amid the down-and-out of eighteenth-century Stockholm live on. Remembered today lyrically as the "Shakespeare of the lute song," he was famous during his lifetime as the king's favorite composer and a singer of bawdy masterpieces on preindustrial Stockholm. The trashy, filthy, still medieval city was home to a hard-drinking people for whom the repression of the Victorian era was distant. Bellman celebrated the common folk who got drunk, drunker, drunkest—and then the clothes came off! Hurrah!

In addition to his lively compositions, Bellman also composed unforgettably beautiful melodies. His most famous song
cycles are *Fredman's Epistler* and *Fredman's Song*, of which
Number 64 ("Winged Butterfly Seen at Haga") is perhaps
one of the most popular pieces. A gentle, pastoral song, it
celebrates Bellman's king and patron, Gustav III, and the
beauty of the royal residence at Haga Park, outside Stockholm.

Winged Butterfly Seen at Haga
O'er the misty park of Haga/In the frosty morning air,/To her
green and fragile dwelling/See the butterfly repair./E'en the
least of tiny creatures,/By the sun and zephyrs warm'd,/Wakes
to new and solemn raptures/In a bed of flowers form'd.
            —translation by Paul Britten Austin.

Popular Exports

When non-Swedes think of music and Sweden, however, it is
unlikely for Taube or Bellman to come to mind but rather
one of the many Swedish pop groups to reach international
fame. ABBA dominated the pop charts in the 1970s; more
recent Swedish musical exports include Roxette, the Cardi-
gans, Robyn, and Ace of Base. And Swedish pop maestro
Max Martin is one of the masterminds responsible for the
success of several American acts, including the Backstreet
Boys and Britney Spears.

Not every Swede cares for ABBA or pop music in general,
but many are proud nonetheless that a country the size of
Sweden can produce stars right alongside the United States
and Great Britain.

Long before the members of ABBA were born, Swedes
were just as proud of world-famous soprano Jenny Lind, the
"Swedish Nightingale," and opera tenor Jussi Björling.

And, of course, we must not forget the impact of Swedes
on the motion picture industry, which goes beyond director

Ingmar Bergman and actresses Greta Garbo and Ingrid Bergman. Today's standouts include director Lasse Hallström, cinematographer Sven Nykvist, and actress Lena Olin, to name just a few award winners. Waves of Swedes have excelled internationally in sports as well. Just as Latin Americans follow their countrymen in American baseball, Swedes follow the feats of Swedish stars in the National Hockey League. Beginning with Björn Borg in the 1970s, a long line of young tennis players has reached the top in international rankings, including Mats Wilander, Stefan Edberg, and Magnus Norman. On the golf course, outstanding Swedes include Jesper Parnevik, Liselotte Neumann, and Annika Sorenstam.

So, although many Swedes find it tiresome that their country's major accomplishments are so often summed up with the names ABBA, Volvo, and Björn Borg, they are still proud that Sweden is recognized abroad for its high-quality exports.

The Blue and Yellow

All over the world, people rally around their national flag to express pride and unity. The Swedes sneer at public manifestations of patriotism centered around bits of cloth. They conveniently forget that they themselves are probably the most flag-flaunting nation of the world,

wrote Peter Berlin in his tongue-in-cheek *The Xenophobe's Guide to the Swedes* (1994, 12). Humorous, yes, but there's some truth to the joke.

Swedes have no equivalent to the Fourth of July, a holiday for which many Americans haul out their flags,[†] but they do love their flag and will fly it on practically any occasion. The

---

[†] Swedish Flag Day, June 6, was established in 1916 and became Sweden's National Day in 1983—not that the Swedes pay any attention.

flag itself, with its sky-blue background and sun-yellow cross, is based on the same pattern as other Scandinavian flags. Unlike the American Stars and Stripes or the British Union Jack, it has no particularly exciting or symbolic history. An early version is believed to have first appeared during the sixteenth century, when it was flown in battle by Swedish warships.

Today, you will find the Swedish flag flying from sailboats and garden flagpoles; printed on postcards, T-shirts, bottles, and cookie tins; and hung in garlands on the branches of Christmas trees. A Midsummer's table, whether in the city or countryside, is not completely set without a couple of miniature flagpoles or flag-printed party napkins.

According to Berlin, "The Swedes are not patriots in the usual sense; for them the national flag is not so much for rallying people to war as an invitation to a picnic" (12).

Indeed, the Swedes' reverence for the flag is more romantic in nature. Some 50 percent of Swedes retreat to summer homes, rented or owned, in the country each year. Whether they are tiny cottages or larger retreats, they will likely feature a spot to raise a flag or wimple for most of the summer, not just on special occasions. The same applies to boats: "The flag belongs in the picture," explained a Swede. "It is part of the ideal summer day." Without the blue and yellow, the atmosphere is just not perfect, and the Swede strives to replicate the ideal.

An Idyll Shattered

In February 1986 Sweden experienced an event that would, in many ways, end its era of peaceful naïveté. Prime Minister Olof Palme was shot and killed on a quiet downtown Stockholm street as he and his wife walked home from an evening movie, without, as was often the case, a bodyguard or other security. Sweden was considered so safe at the time that heads of state eschewed the precautions and protections taken in other countries. Before Palme's assassination, it was almost unfathomable to consider such an act occurring in Sweden, a bastion of security, social order, and peace.

Touring Scandinavia twelve years after the killing, *New York Times* columnist Warren Hoge quoted a Swedish diplomat who said, "When Palme was killed, we were an innocent, virgin country." The "idyllic and ideal" modern nation was suddenly thrown into a much harsher reality (1998).

The last twenty years have seen other aspects of national pride splinter as well. As have other European countries and the United States, Sweden has experienced an increase in racist and white-supremacist activity. Intolerant behavior once thought to be absolutely "un-Swedish" is increasingly being manifested—and transmitted, thanks to the global reach of the Internet.

A minority of young Swedish men are wrapping themselves in the flag of Sweden's last imperialist king, King Karl XII, and demanding that the white Swedish "race" be preserved. Because these sentiments seem to be most prevalent among young, working-class men, some attribute racist activity to increased immigration to Sweden. These individuals may see their employment or living situations worsening and blame it on immigrants. Other observers, however, credit evil of an earlier vintage: lingering Nazism and antisemitism among older individuals who stand in the shadows and support these networks. In either case, Swedes abhor the connection of their flag to racist or fascist movements—a brutal violation of the Swedes' nationalromantik and love of country.

5

The Individual and the Group: Self-Sufficiency and Solidarity

Bra karl klarar sig själv.
(*A good man manages on his own.*)
Ensam är stark.
(*One is strong on one's own.*)

—Swedish proverbs

Summary: Swedes, like Americans, view themselves as independent individuals. For the Swede, independence is linked directly to one's sense of self-sufficiency. Part of being self-sufficient means solving problems for oneself. It is important for the Swede to see her- or himself as *duktig*, or capable. The corollary of the Swede's self-sufficiency is an aversion to indebtedness. Swedes are raised with the idea that people derive a strong sense of security from being part of a group, which in turn allows them to develop into strong and independent individuals. Non-Swedes, however, sometimes misinterpret the Swedes' emphasis on social conformity and on their social-welfare system as evidence of a collectivist culture. This is not necessarily the case.

Swedes, like Americans, view themselves as independent

individuals, but being independent has a different meaning in each culture. For example, an American may wonder how Swedes can be independent while also being subject to considerable pressure to be part of the group. An understanding of Swedish independence depends on understanding the role of the group or organization in Swedish life, a role that has developed alongside the implementation of the Swedish Model.

Understanding the Swedes' sense of independence and how it relates to protecting their privacy can prevent foreigners from misinterpreting uncomfortable silences and refusals of offers for help as impoliteness. To an American, being independent usually means being the captain of one's ship, free to pursue one's interests and seek one's fortune. It also implies action on some level. When Americans speak of their rights, they are often referring to noninterference of the government, the freedom to pursue opportunities, and a chance for personal achievement and success. This is the right of the individual—life, liberty, and the pursuit of happiness.

In Sweden the concept of independence is interpreted a bit differently. To be independent means not to be dependent upon or indebted to another person. The Swedish sense of independence has a more passive quality than the American one does. Rather than the opportunity to succeed, the chance to be self-sufficient is what is important. One might say *the American wants the freedom to do, while the Swede wants the freedom to be.*

Insistence on Self-Sufficiency

Swedish children learn at a very young age that it is good to be able to do things for themselves. When presented with the image of the strong Swede, a burly Viking may come to the American imagination. For the Swede, however, strength has more to do with self-sufficiency than with physical prowess.

Having a strong constitution and the ability to deal with a variety of situations in a calm, capable, and quiet fashion is highly valued in both men and women.

In many other cultures, by way of contrast, stronger emphasis is placed on interdependence within the family unit and community. In many Asian or Latin American families, for example, children typically live in their parents' home until they marry, and extended families may also live under one roof.

In Sweden, on the other hand, moving away from the immediate family can happen as early as age sixteen. For example, it is not uncommon for students in remote, rural areas to have to travel hundreds of miles to attend high school; they live on their own or share apartments with other teenage students during the week and commute home on the weekends. An eighteen-year-old is generally considered an adult and capable of living on his or her own permanently.

High unemployment during the early to mid-1990s forced some young people to live with their parents longer, worrying some Swedes that the younger generations were growing up to be too dependent, having never had the chance to stand on their own feet.

Self-sufficiency even carries over into marriage: many Swedish couples keep separate bank accounts for husband and wife, allowing people to retain a measure of financial independence even in the most committed of personal relationships.

As Americans maintain their privacy by protecting their space (e.g., big cars, privacy fences, gated communities), Swedes maintain their privacy by remaining quiet. Swedes are generally slow to divulge personal information, particularly when it comes to sharing problems. Many are even reluctant to do so with close family members and friends. Part of being self-sufficient means solving problems for oneself— even if one could benefit from help. This also leads to a strongly negative view of people who collect unwarranted benefits. No one looks down on the handicapped or elderly or others who legitimately need assistance. Immigrants who collect social benefits, however, without looking as if they need them—need, after all, isn't always visible on the sur-face—can be singled out for suspicion.

The ideal that one should take care of ones' own problems is so strong that it can feel demeaning for some Swedes to accept outside help. As a result, "it is very difficult to do a favor for a Swedish person," said an American man with a son and former sambo in Sweden. "It has to do with their being very self-sufficient, all the time, in every aspect of their lives. They insist upon it." His former partner followed what he called the "unwritten and unspoken" law of never bothering a neighbor or stranger with one's problems. And this has everything to do with privacy and self-sufficiency: "One should always take care of things oneself. I found...this exas-perating," he said. "On my own, I have found Swedes very helpful, where they could be, with any questions or problems I may have needed help with."

One Swede good-naturedly shared a story about a visit by a French couple living in Sweden. As the three of them left his apartment, he paused to close the door behind them:

> When we were leaving, I stood and fiddled with the lock on the outer door a moment. [The French couple] said they were surprised I couldn't manage to lock the door; after all, it was a "Swedish lock." "A Swedish lock? What's that?" I asked them. As it turns out, that was their expression for a lock that doesn't require a key to lock; you can simply close the door behind you when you leave. But if you've left your keys inside, you're in trouble! I asked them why they called this a Swedish lock. They laughed, then said, "Being locked out is probably the only way you Swedes ever talk to your neigh-bors!" What could I say? They were right.

Because Swedes find it important not to impose on others, they may not be as quick to ask other people whether they have problems or whether something is wrong. As a result, Swedes may sometimes seem to people from more obviously intimate cultures to be aloof, uninterested, or even callous. One of the authors relates a recent situation that demonstrates this point. Upon arriving in Sweden at Stockholm's Arlanda Airport, she found herself impeding progress on one of the terminal's escalators with her rolling luggage cart and other belongings. A young Swedish couple entered the escalator behind her, and she offered to let them pass. They politely declined. As the escalator neared the top, the author struggled with her cart when something on it got caught between the steps. With some difficulty, she managed to extricate herself and exit. All the while, the couple looked on in silence.

Some time later it struck her: the Swedish couple had not made any effort to assist her, although she was certain that had the same situation occurred in the United States, someone would likely have volunteered to lend a hand.

The Swedes had probably felt embarrassed for her and didn't want to invade her privacy (and thus increase her embarrassment) at such an awkward moment, explained a Swede upon hearing the story. It doesn't necessarily mean they didn't care. "If she needed help, all she had to do was ask, and someone would certainly have helped her immediately. Otherwise, they would assume she wanted to be left alone," he said. It is an explanation that makes sense but may still not satisfy non-Swedes.

Swedish ethnologist Åke Daun speculates that some of this reluctance to become involved in others' problems or involve others in one's own is based on the Swedes' desire to be *duktig* above all else (1996). To be duktig means to do a good job, to be responsible and capable, to be well behaved, or to accomplish something independently. *Duktig* is a word that carries strong emotional overtones: children who behave well are duktig; adults who are talented and independent are duktig. Someone who locks himself out of his own apartment or has to ask others for help in general is not duktig. Had the Swedish couple on the escalator rushed to help the author with her cart without her asking, that might have implied that she was not duktig.

The fear of making a fool of oneself is related to the importance of being duktig. Daun and others speculate that this is, in part, the reason for the Swedes' reticence in other situations as well. If Swedes don't know the people they are talking to, or if they have to express themselves in English, they are afraid that they will not appear duktig. Of course, many Americans have the same desire to be capable and the same dread of making fools of themselves as do the Swedes. In Sweden, however, it seems to have risen to the level of a national character trait.

Squaring Up

The corollary of the Swedes' penchant for self-sufficiency is an aversion to indebtedness. Swedes feel that *man ska alltid vara kvitt*—you should always be "squared up" with others, not owing anyone anything.

Many a foreigner has commented on the frequency with which the Swedes say thank you, to an almost ridiculous degree, a behavior related to their sense of reciprocity. If you do something for a Swede, he or she will be grateful but will also feel obligated to return the favor in order to restore equilibrium. Saying thank you fulfills part of that obligation. Couples inviting another couple over for dinner will expect a return invitation in due time. People who meet on the street are sure to thank each other for the last time they visited each other's home, even if the event occurred weeks earlier.

Similarly, Swedes are not as comfortable with the idea of "treating" others to dinner out or having others treat them. In Sweden, everyone is assumed to have similar resources, so it seems inappropriate to pay for someone else. "This is not a common thing to do in Sweden," reported an American woman living there. "In a country where most married couples still have separate bank accounts and sambos still split dinner bills, you don't normally do this or even offer, even in the most small sense, for instance, buying a cup of coffee for someone."

She found this to be quite different from socializing in the United States. "We normally treated our close friends for dinner; the next one would be on them. But it didn't have to be the same amount [of money], nor was that even thought about," she says.

Another American shared the story of a Swedish friend in an amorous relationship with a younger Swedish woman. The friend invited the young woman to fly to New York City with him for a romantic weekend. "She declined and told him she didn't have the cash. He offered to pay. And she said no— because then she would owe him money!"

This attitude illustrates the Swedes' preference for avoiding reciprocity—even at the cost of missing a free trip to New York. As the American woman above hastens to add, stories like this should not be interpreted to mean that Swedes are stingy or ungenerous. Swedes can and do borrow from or lend money to good friends, of course. They simply expect to be paid back promptly and in exact amounts. In Sweden, fair is square.

"Organized" Sweden

Swedes are raised with the idea that the individual derives a strong sense of security from being part of a group, which in turn allows him or her to develop into a strong and independent individual. In addition to "belonging" to their nationality, many if not most Swedes naturally join many other groups during their lifetime. There is even a term for this phenomenon: *Organisationssverige* ("organized" Sweden). Although the concept has its roots in the labor and social movements, Sweden has become a land of organizations in general.

"Everyone seems to belong to an association," said an American married to a Swede. Associations, which seem to be present in every aspect of life, include sports clubs; temperance societies; study circles; civic organizations; political and religious organizations; parents' associations; consumer cooperatives; farmers' unions; cultural associations; and bird-watching, photography, and sailing clubs. In 1992 Swedes were, on average, members of 2.9 different associations. Fifty-one percent of the population considered itself "active" in one or more associations, and 29 percent held some kind of elected position. In adult education alone, 37 percent of women and 28 percent of men reported participating in a study circle or taking a course during the past year (Statistics Sweden 2000).

"The Swedes seems to begin their 'organizational' life at around age thirteen, and there they learn to follow the very democratic procedures they will use throughout their lives," the American said. Solidarity as a value is thereby introduced early. Americans certainly enjoy group activities as well, but for many of them, clubs and organizations function as a place to shine and an opportunity to increase their social visibility through leadership positions. For the Swede, the club is above all a safe place to socialize and grow.

Thus, working as a team comes naturally and early to the Swedes as well, an important factor in the success of the Swedish Model. Teamwork, however, dates back to well before the modern reinvention of Swedish society. Sweden's location in a harsh climate with long, dark winters made it imperative for people to work together to survive. Because the country was almost entirely agrarian until the beginning of the twentieth century, life depended on the ability to work in teams. According to Åke Daun, "Farms in Sweden depended upon each other for all sorts of cooperative labor: maintenance of fences, harvesting crops, haying, helping each other with house building and with various other economic contingencies" (1996, 208).

The Swedes' ability to work together effectively is evident in a variety of areas, including the Swedish cooperative movement, which was first examined in detail in the classic *Sweden: The Middle Way on Trial*, by Marquis Childs in 1947. How the cooperative movement was organized sheds some light on how Swedes have worked toward a common goal with the aim of benefiting the group:

In Sweden those who were interested in promoting better housing had also come to the realization two decades or more ago that there would be little real progress until the interest of the group to benefit from improved housing was enlisted. And this, it may be noted here, is at the root of most of the reforms that Sweden has adopted; they are *sui generis*, growing out of a social need that has been keenly felt and insistently presented against a broad background of social and economic education; they have not, in short, been superimposed from above through beneficence or the righteousness of a class that took its own superiority for granted. This is a vital distinction, and it has led in Sweden, more often than not, to the cooperative solution of social and economic problems (51).

But none of this cooperative spirit argues against the archetype of the strong and autonomous Swede, either. The Swedes would assert that only a society of strong and self-sufficient individuals—with sympathy and solidarity for those who are not—could accomplish the reforms that their nation has.

It is tempting to conclude that Swedes, although self-sufficient, are a collective people. This conclusion is easily drawn from the "social" aspects of Swedish social democracy, which are, indeed, collective in nature. Social democracy stresses protecting the weak and vulnerable. Folkhemmet, as we have discussed, suggests that the society, just like the family, should take care of all its members, weak or strong. Also, the Swedes' preference for avoiding conflict and their consensus-based decision making, two character traits that will be discussed in upcoming chapters, can be interpreted as collective behavior by people from cultures with other dominant values.

"Feminine" versus "Masculine"

Rather than individualism versus collectivism, the difference non-Swedes perceive is more likely what organizational psychologist Geert Hofstede describes as the "feminine" versus the "masculine" in cultures. Sweden, like the United States and Great Britain, for example, has a society in which the individual is very important. But Sweden, unlike the others, is also feminine—in fact, the most feminine country in the world, by Hofstede's definition. In others words, it is no accident that Sweden is sometimes referred to as *Moder Svea* (Mother Sweden).

Hofstede's masculine-feminine dimension does not refer to individuals behaving in a "macho" versus an "effeminate" manner (despite what some immigrants to Sweden may think about men who like to cook and care for children). Instead, masculine and feminine refer to the range of values that are desirable in a society. Masculinity refers to societies

in which social gender roles are clearly distinct (i.e., men are supposed to be assertive, tough and focused on material success, whereas women are supposed to be more modest, tender and concerned with the quality of life); femininity pertains to societies in which social gender roles overlap (i.e., both men and women are supposed to be modest, tender and concerned with the quality of life). (1991, 84)

Thus, assertive behavior is valued in masculine countries, while modest behavior is valued in feminine countries. In feminine countries both boys and girls learn to be modest and noncompetitive; assertive behavior and attempts to excel, as we will discuss later on, are easily ridiculed. Masculine countries, such as the United States, strive for a competitive, performance-based society, at the expense of some of their citizens; whereas feminine countries, such as Sweden, opt for a welfare society, where everyone is cared for. Caring for others is one of the basic tenets of the Swedish Model.

Values of Feminine and Masculine Societies Contrasted (Hofstede 1991)

Feminine: Sweden, Norway, Denmark, Finland, The Netherlands	Masculine: United States, Japan, Great Britain, Italy, Austria, Switzerland
Dominant values in society are caring for others and preservation	Dominant values in society are material success and progress
Everybody is supposed to be modest	Men are supposed to be assertive, ambitious, and tough
Sympathy for the weak	Sympathy for the strong
Work in order to live	Live in order to work
Managers use intuition and strive for consensus	Managers are expected to be decisive and assertive
Resolution of conflicts by compromise and negotiation	Resolution of conflicts by fighting them out
Stress on equality, solidarity, and quality of work life	Stress on equity, competition among colleagues, and performance

Individualism versus Conformity

What is more difficult to discover is how Swedes manage to retain their individualism when faced with the conformity expected of them by their culture. It is worthwhile, then, to briefly compare the Swedish and American views of conformity.

Americans do not typically believe that they should be like other Americans. This is easy to understand considering the diversity of the population. As a result, many Americans, instead, identify themselves based on the values and beliefs of specific subgroups, such as political parties, ethnic groups, or religious denominations. They then conform to the norms for these subgroups, under an overarching "American" umbrella.

In a small country like Sweden, however, where the population up until the last few decades was ethnically and socially homogeneous, it is much easier for a standardized, national norm to evolve. As a result of this tendency, however, there is intolerance for people who fall outside the parameters of this norm.

In chapter 7 we will discuss the concept of the Law of Jante, which reminds Scandinavians not to think of themselves as better than anyone else. This proscription places a high premium on conformity, the concept of being like everyone else. In fact you will frequently hear a Swede describe her- or himself as just *en vanlig Svensson*, an ordinary Svensson. This is considered a modest, positive statement.

Shedding light on the Swedes' complex view of conformity, sociologist Birger Beckman, in *Lasternas Bok* (*The Book of Vices*), discusses the Swedes' tendency to conform to the group by comparing tolerance in Swedes with tolerance in Italians. Whereas Swedes appear more tolerant of others in what they consider private, moral matters, such as religion, politics, or sexual preference, they are less tolerant of individuals who look or behave differently. The opposite views were found in Italy, where moral issues were important, but individual idiosyncrasies were accepted and considered normal. To the Swede your religion and sexual orientation are seen as private and not of great interest, but standing out in dress or demeanor takes on greater significance.

Although *Lasternas Bok* was written more than fifty years ago, it still rings true and may help explain the Swedes' views toward immigrants today. Newcomers are encouraged to maintain their cultural practices and languages at home, but at the same time, are expected to adapt to Swedish everyday behavior. If they don't conform to Swedish behavioral norms, they will have a hard time being accepted. According to Beckman, this tendency to conform to "a Swedish ideal" has both advantages and disadvantages. On the plus side, conformity has been useful politically in enabling the country to evolve without the violent opposition or unrest experienced by countries with more diverse populations. On the downside, it can expose individuals who don't conform to severe social pressure or even ostracism (1946). Much attention has been paid in Sweden over the last ten years to the subject of *mobbning* (bullying). Mobbning refers to situations where individuals are harassed or ostracized by co-workers or schoolmates, sometimes to the point that the individuals suffer health problems, develop mental illnesses, or even commit suicide. Mobbning does not refer to the everyday tensions and confrontations of the schoolyard or workplace but to more systematic, long-term physical or psychological abuse. The government has taken steps to improve enforcement of laws against this kind of behavior. Swedish culture breeds expectations of conformity, but at the same time folkhemmet guarantees safety and security for everyone. Above all, mobbning is a direct attack on the Swedish premise of individualism: the freedom *to be*.

Socialistic Individualism

So, is Sweden a country of individuals or groups? Both. Swedes are willing to act as a group to safeguard the rights of the individual, a concept Swedish political scientist Bo Rothstein has referred to as "socialistic individualism." "There's a sense that the presence of certain institutions creates a level of security for all citizens that paradoxically also creates more freedom," explained Brian Palmer, Ph.D., an anthropologist and faculty member in the department of religion at Harvard University (2001).

"Abstract expressions of the freedom of the individual in Anglo-American tradition often take the form that one should be free to do what one wants as long as it does not harm others," Palmer said. "I think the second part of that phrase—'as long as it does not harm others'—is not taken as seriously as it should be in the United States." The Swedes follow roughly the same paradigm, he noted, but are willing to take a harder look at whether an individual's behavior is, in fact, good for the group at large—and thus for other individuals.

As the Swedes see it, according to Palmer, "there is more freedom [for individuals] in a society where one knows he or she won't become homeless, where one can send one's eight-year-old daughter to a movie at night without worrying that she will be assaulted or hit by a car, where one can drink the water and breathe the air" and know he or she is safe.

6

The Lagom Phenomenon

Lagom är bäst!
(*"Just right"* is best! or, *Everything in moderation.*)
För mycket och för litet skämmer allt.
(*Too much and too little spoils everything.*)
— Swedish proverbs

Summary: The Swedes have captured the essence of taking the "middle way" with the concept of lagom, "everything in moderation." Unlike in the United States, however, where moderation is most frequently applied to indulgences such as food or drink, lagom in Sweden applies to life in general: how much one eats, drinks, works, spends, owns. One should eat enough, but not too much, work hard, but not too hard, have enough, but not too much. Lagom makes sense to the Swedes but can be chafing for Americans, raised in a culture where "too much is never enough."

To understand the Swedes, one must have an appreciation for the concept of lagom. The word *lagom* (pronounced "LAW-gohm") has no exact equivalent in English. According to the Swedish-English dictionaries, it means "enough," "sufficient," "adequate," "fitting," "appropriate," or "suitable," but a better translation is "everything in moderation." It is easy to understand lagom's usefulness and appeal to the Swedes, who love "the middle way," that which is "just right." Where does the concept of lagom come from? Legend has it that the Vikings met in assemblies and concluded each meeting by sharing a bowl of mead, an alcoholic honey wine. The drinking vessel was passed from man to man with the understanding that no one should drink too much; in other words, one should be sure to leave enough for everybody as the bowl went laget om, meaning "around the group." Thus, the shortened word lagom emerged to describe this collectively enforced restraint and moderation.

There is no way to prove the truth of this bit of Swedish folklore. However, if you were to pick just one word to describe the Swedish mentality, it would have to be lagom. Anyone who spent his or her formative years in Sweden learned early on that lagom är bäst—lagom is best. This is especially important for Americans to remember, as the implied restraint of lagom contrasts sharply with the expansive American notion that "too much is never enough." In Sweden overindulgence is frowned upon. Lagom in this way dovetails with the Lutheran moral codes that have influenced the Swedish mentality. The ideals of modesty and humility can certainly be traced to this religious heritage. The Hávamál, with which we opened the first chapter of this book, also has much to say that supports the concept of lagom. It is full of advice such as "be hospitable, but not too hospitable"; "be wise, but not too wise"; "enjoy beer, but don't drink too much"; and "take care not to boast over your sharp intellect."

In Culture Shock, author Charlotte Rosen Svensson deftly defines lagom as "one should work hard but not too hard, and eat enough but not too much, and have enough money but not too much" (Svensson 1996, 51).

Swedes relocating to the United States are frequently surprised by the array of choices presented in the grocery stores. It is not unusual to hear them ask, "Why do you need so many brands of every item?" To some, it seems excessive and makes no practical sense; in other words, it violates lagom. The American, on the other hand, loves to have choices and may find Swedish grocery stores limited in selection. That is changing, however, as "mega" supermarkets pop up across Europe, including Sweden.

Portion sizes in restaurants are another matter for lagom thinking. The Swedish norm is to put on your plate only what you can finish. To be served a large portion that you will clearly be unable to finish is considered wasteful in Sweden; in the United States, it may instead be viewed as "good value for the money." High prices make eating out far less common in Sweden than in the U.S. Swedes usually eat their meals at home, especially dinner, and they are often careful to use the leftovers. Older Swedes in particular, only a generation or two removed from much leaner times, are not yet conditioned to the throwaway attitude so often found in the U.S. We say *yet*, because this attitude is changing. Young people in Sweden today are adopting more and more aspects of American culture, including greater consumption.

The word *lagom* is commonly used as a modifier in Swedish: an exotic dish may be lagom spicy; a glass of beer, lagom cold; the weather, lagom warm. For the Swede, it is as if there is an invisible point on any continuum where everything is as it should be. It may not be possible for a non-Swede to completely absorb lagom, because it requires an innate sense of "just rightness" that is difficult to acquire as an adult.

Like other aspects of culture, lagom is a value that Swedes absorb as children. The easiest place to teach it seems to be at the dinner table. Asked to explain the meaning of lagom, an eleven-year-old Swedish boy said, "If you were eating [boiled] potatoes and you took twenty, that would be too much. Five would be too few. But ten or twelve would be lagom."

These are very small Swedish new potatoes (or one very hungry little boy) we're talking about! But his definition of lagom is clear: restrain yourself; there must be enough for everyone. Swedish children are admonished not to take more food than they can finish, not to fill the glass of juice too full. They learn that lagom is something that can be measured. But lagom is taught in less tangible ways as well. As we'll discuss more in chapter 7 on *Jantelagen*, Swedish children are sometimes subtly discouraged from flying too high. An American child's dream of becoming president, however unlikely to be fulfilled, may still be positively reinforced; meanwhile, a Swedish child may be told such dreams are unrealistic and encouraged to think more practically. Swedes are more likely to teach their children to keep both feet firmly planted on the ground and not stray too far into fantasy.

An American journalist who worked in Sweden described Swedes as born with an internal ruler that enables them to measure lagom instinctively. Fortunately, they are usually forgiving of the embarrassing mistakes and oversteppings of outsiders; they reserve their harshest judgment for themselves.

For Americans and other people who strive for everything biggest, most, and best, and for whom "the sky is the limit," the Swedish desire for lagom may seem very limiting, very unambitious. Lagom is average. Lagom is...well, lagom.

There are, of course, areas where the Swedes are anything but moderate, as in their tendency toward binge drinking, particularly among young people. As one Swede explained it, "If you can handle your job without anyone knowing you were drunk the night before, it's not excessive." In other words, it does not upset the balance of lagom. More benign passions include candy and coffee—Swedes come close to leading the world in per capita consumption of both.

Lagom at Work

Unlike in the United States, where the expression "everything in moderation" is typically applied to areas of hedonistic overindulgence (e.g., eating, drinking, smoking, sex), in Sweden lagom is a concept applied to life in general, including work. With the Swedes' basic belief that "lagom is best," potential is rife for misunderstandings among international colleagues.

Charles Hampden-Turner and Alfons Trompenaars, in *The Seven Cultures of Capitalism*, define lagom as "a search for a mean between the individual and society." When the attempt to reach a mutual agreement, or consensus, is achieved, it means that an optimal position somewhere between the opinions expressed has been reached—the lagom point, if you will (1993, 253). In one Swedish multinational company, lagom became such an issue that the American managers coined the word "lagomize" to describe the situation of having to regroup to find the lagom point. (The importance of consensus decision making will be discussed in greater detail in Chapter 12 on doing business in Sweden.)

In addition to its connection with consensus, lagom also guides the act of working itself. "Apart from the Swedes' way of communicating, this has been the hardest thing for me, as an American, to handle and figure out about the Swedes," said an American man regarding his efforts to start his own business in Sweden. "Americans are full of entrepreneurial spirit. The Swedes are not. I ran smack-dab, straight-on, head-first into lagom like hitting a brick wall with a car." For him, lagom meant that the Swedes he worked with weren't willing to put in the same hours that he was in order to get the business on its feet—his way of measuring their enthusiasm and commitment to the project.

An article on Sweden in *National Geographic* magazine noted that

some Swedes fear that the lagom ethic, combined with an educational system that stresses uniformity, discourages the best and the brightest—the smartest kid in the class, the entrepreneur, the risk taker, the artist, the inventor—in short, the very kinds of people Sweden needs now, more than ever to succeed. (Belt 1993, 22)

As a result, Sweden has feared a "brain drain" of talented people to other countries. Swedes pride themselves on being hard workers. Swedes working in U.S. companies often comment that Americans spend too much time with a coffee cup in hand, visiting with co-workers; thus, although Americans work long hours, they don't work efficiently. (This impression also comes from the fact that Swedes take breaks in a more formal manner—they stop work to take coffee, whereas Americans take informal breaks that look like work, such as walking around and chatting with colleagues.)

Americans, on the other hand, may tend to view the Swedes as antisocial or lacking commitment. A common complaint of foreign businesspeople working in Sweden is that their local colleagues are likely to stop working and leave at the end of the day, even if an important project has not been completed. An American often feels compelled to work late to get things done, whereas the Swede generally feels entitled to go home.

Because lagom implies balance, spending too many hours on the job is not lagom to the Swede, although Swedes are finding themselves putting in longer and longer hours now. He or she believes that there is a time for work and a time for family and leisure. Most Swedish employers believe that time for "R&R" is critical for increased effectiveness and productivity. This can be important for international employers to remember. When an American or British executive works long hours, leaving little time for himself or his family, he is often seen by his employer as ambitious. In Sweden, on the other hand, a tendency to "overwork" may actually be perceived as evidence of inefficiency or an inability to prioritize.

In an event that would have been unheard-of in the United States, former Swedish Prime Minister Ingvar Carlsson decided to leave office in the middle of his term because he wanted to spend more time with his family—and he is widely believed to have been telling the truth.

Lagom is applied not only to time on the job but also to the money earned there. Although chief executives of Swedish companies often make substantial salaries, their compensation is nowhere near the earnings of many top U.S. executives. From a Swedish perspective, great disparities in salary are simply not fair and definitely not lagom. High salaries are heavily taxed to reduce these disparities.

Even Sweden's more conservative political parties agree with left-wing Social Democrats on this point. Extremely high wages for executives can create problems for negotiators with the country's powerful trade unions—and what is a union if not the enforcement of lagom?

The Confederation of Swedish Enterprises (Svenskt Näringsliv), which represents business owners in Sweden, went so far as to assert that Sweden can't handle more than "very modest, nominal wage increases," even in a booming economy. As a result, Swedish executives working for American companies, uncomfortable with asking for what they regard to be astronomical salaries, have been known to retain American professionals to negotiate their compensation packages. A Swede will be quick to point out that money is not always the top consideration for Swedes when accepting a position. For example, someone may seek a new position simply because it offers an opportunity to work with interesting people or to learn something new.

Lagom can also have an impact in sales. The American approach to selling oneself or a product by using whatever means necessary to stand out from the competition is not something the Swede feels comfortable doing. American marketing methods, particularly self-promotion, are seen as excessive and viewed with distrust by many Swedes, as we will discuss in chapter 7 on another fundamental Swedish concept, Jantelagen.

As for pricing of items or services, it is important to know that there is usually little room for negotiation with a Swede. They are much less likely to engage in bargaining because they believe that they have determined what the lagom, or fair, price is already.

Lagom and Society

In *Understanding Global Cultures*, Martin J. Gannon and Associates state that lagom is also the key to understanding the rationale behind Sweden's political philosophy of social democracy, a "merging of the ideals of socialism and capitalism" (Gannon and Associates 1994, 109).

The political continuum in the United States represents a broad range of views: there are "bleeding-heart liberals" to the far left, "fundamentalist conservatives" to the far right, with the Democrats and Republicans huddled in the center. In Sweden most political parties operate closer the center, in a sort of lagom zone. Some party ideologies lie to the left or right of center, but extremism itself flies in the face of lagom. Still, the lagom zone lies far, far to the left of the American center; the most conservative Swedish politician would be seen at least as a Democrat, if not further left, in the U.S.

Lagom is also related to the sense of "unemotional practicality" whereby the Swedes believe all problems can be solved through logical reasoning. Lagom makes sense because it is fair, balanced, and logical. Lagom ensures that everyone has enough and nobody goes without. By discussing an issue rationally, a lagom point can always be reached. Because this method has been very successful for a long period of time, Swedes continue to feel that it is the ideal approach to problem solving. They don't understand why others seem to get caught up in emotional debates that often seem to lead nowhere.

As discussed elsewhere, Sweden has long been rather homogeneous culturally, particularly compared with the multicultural United States. It is obviously much easier to be "of one mind" when most people have grown up with very similar values and beliefs. This fact has become increasingly apparent to the Swedes in recent decades, during which a large number of immigrants have settled in Sweden, constantly putting lagom to the test.

Given the prominent role of lagom, how is it enforced in Swedish society? That is the job of Jantelagen, the big psychological stick that keeps everyone in his or her place. More on that in the next chapter.

7

Jantelagen: Who Do You Think You Are?

Jantelagen (The Law of Jante)

Du skall inte tro att du är något.
Thou shalt not presume that thou art someone.
Du skall inte tro att du är lika god som vi.
Thou shalt not presume that thou art as good as we.
Du skall inte tro att du är klokare än vi.
Thou shalt not presume that thou art any wiser than we.
Du skall inte inbilla dig att du är bättre än vi.
Thou shalt never indulge in the conceit of imagining that thou art better than we.
Du skall inte tro att du vet mera än vi.
Thou shalt not presume that thou art more knowledgeable than we.
Du skall inte tro att du är förmer än vi.
Thou shalt not presume that thou art more [important] than we.
Du skall inte tro att du duger till något.
Thou shalt not presume that thou art going to amount to anything.
Du skall inte skratta åt oss.
Thou art not entitled to laugh at us.
Du skall inte tro att några bryr sig om dig.
Thou shalt never imagine that anyone cares about thee.

82

Du skall inte tro att du kan lära oss något.
Thou shalt not suppose that thou can teach us anything.
—from *A Refugee Crosses His Tracks*, Aksel Sandemose
(1899–1965)

Summary: Jantelagen is a Scandinavian concept with the underlying theme of societally enforced humility and self-restraint. Expressed as a series of commandments, Jantelagen attempts to "keep people in their place" by discouraging vanity of any kind. One consequence of Jantelagen is the "Royal Swedish Envy"—there is a tendency to envy and thus criticize anyone who appears to be "too successful." Observers have seen Jantelagen as a threat to Sweden's global competitiveness by potentially discouraging innovation and achievement. But younger Swedes seem to be leaving Jante in their wake as they lead Sweden into the information-technology-based global economy.

Every culture has hidden rules, its silent code of social conduct, and these rules are often codified in a nation's literature and folklore.

Generations of Americans, for example, have been guided by Benjamin Franklin's common-sense aphorisms in *Poor Richard's Almanac:* "Early to bed and early to rise makes a man healthy, wealthy and wise." "Little strokes fell great oaks." "He who lies down with dogs gets up with fleas."

Scandinavia, too, has a rich tradition of proverbs, legends, and folklore that serve as culture-forming texts. But among them is a list of ten "commandments" commonly referred to in Swedish as *Jantelagen* and coined by Danish-Norwegian author Aksel Sandemose in his 1933 book, *A Refugee Crosses His Tracks.* The book is set in the fictional town of Jante, a narrow-minded community based on Sandemose's Danish hometown of Nykøbing. It bitterly describes the ugly side of small-town mentality. Jantelagen, or "Law of Jante," has come to signify the unspoken rules and jealousies of this mindset. Although scholars maintain that Sandemose was indeed writing about Nykøbing, readers across Denmark, Norway, and Sweden identified so closely with Jantelagen that many were convinced the author was writing about their own communities. This same reaction can be observed in more hierarchical, class-driven societies when one tries to move "beyond one's station." The difference is that in these societies, people find a certain comfort in knowing where they belong in the hierarchy; Swedes find a certain comfort in knowing (or at least believing) that there is no hierarchy. The underlying themes of Jantelagen are humility and self-restraint. Self-promotion, boasting, and expressions of vanity are not permitted, regardless of one's accomplishments or talents. It is the extreme manifestation of the Swede's natural tendency toward modesty and equality: the idea that being different, particularly if it means being *better than others*, is not something to boast about.

Although relatively recent in origin, Jantelagen crystallized beliefs long existing in Scandinavian society. It reflects the emphasis of living within accepted boundaries and not drawing attention to oneself. In the 1940s researcher Birger Beckman explained that the Swede becomes anxious if anything occurs outside his or her acceptable framework. One should think and believe like everyone else. One should not differ from the group but live according to the norms of society. Watching someone flout Jantelagen is extremely uncomfortable for the observer—it is a threat to the established order of things, casting doubt on one's own position (1946).

Interestingly, although Sandemose's novel was set in a Danish town, the Swedes seem to have taken Jantelagen closer to heart than either the Danes or the Norwegians. *Janteloven*, as the set of laws is known in those two countries, is recognized as a cultural millstone but perceived much less often as a continuing problem. Marc Bünger, an American management consultant with Swedish-owned Icon Medialab in San Francisco, who has worked with people from all three nations, suggests that the individual "personality" of each country explains why Jantelagen/loven has a different level of power. The Scandinavian countries, he says, are like three sisters:

> Sweden is the oldest sister, very tall with long blonde hair, prim, proper, elegant, and refined. Norway is the middle sister, the natural one with straight brown hair and no make-up, wearing a wool sweater and picking berries. Denmark is the rebellious little sister with green hair who is always getting into trouble and making her parents crazy, but she's just as smart as the other two. (2000)

As the most straightlaced culture of the three, Bünger says, Swedish culture takes Jantelagen (and itself, for that matter) more seriously, while Danish culture, more continental and cantankerous, flouts it.

But even the Danes will sneer at someone who drives a Jaguar around town, said a Swede who worked in Copenhagen (and drove a Jaguar). And a Danish friend's son told his mother that when his college application form asked for his father's profession, he wrote "worker" rather than "dentist," for the latter seemed to him too snobbish.

Norway, which was controlled by Denmark or Sweden for centuries, falls somewhere in between. As we will note later in the chapter, Norwegians still feel sensitive about the effects of Jantelagen/loven. But they are already slightly more hierarchical than the Swedes. For example, a Swedish physician who has worked in Norway noted that physicians there are more hierarchical than in Sweden. Norwegian doctors are more likely to draw a distinction between themselves and other people, she said, through titles and social status. That may not be a flattering example, but it does reflect an environment where some poppies are taller than others, to borrow the Australian metaphor. Yet even Norway stands in stark contrast to the United States, where setting oneself apart is not only accepted but desirable.

Some non-Swedes confuse Jantelagen with *lagom*. They are certainly related but are not the same. Although *lagom*, as discussed in the previous chapter, also has to do with modesty and self-restraint, it is a neutral concept; Jantelagen, on the other hand, is personal and controlling. Other cultures include similar proscriptions. In Japan "a nail that sticks up is hammered down." In Australia "tall poppies" are snipped down to size.

"Jantelagen is an expression of small people's desire to put their neighbors in their place," wrote Swedish economist Bengt Valdemarsson (1997). But it functions on the macro level as well, he argued, simply by substituting the government for the community "we" of Sandemose's original treatise. For example, "Thou shalt not presume that thou art as good as the state" and "Thou shalt never presume that the state cares about thee." With Sweden's system of progressive taxation in mind, Valdemarsson added an eleventh commandment: "Thou shalt not presume that what you earn is thine." This sentiment is particularly strong in the Swedish business community.

Impact on Individuals

Although few Swedes will tell you that Jantelagen is a good thing, its effects persist. Swedes internalize the concept from a very early age: don't boast about yourself; let your actions speak for themselves. Swedes are not known for giving compliments because many are so uncomfortable accepting them themselves. Although a compliment based on an accomplishment is appreciated, the typical response may be to brush it off with, "It was really nothing" or "That's just my job."

Ironically, the more successful or independent the person, the greater the potential for guilt. Swedes follow the lives of their sports stars and celebrities in the newspapers with as much interest as people in any Western country, and they are equally proud of them. However, even very popular and famous Swedes may find themselves to be the objects of mild to serious public scorn if they are observed to be presenting themselves as better than others or beyond the reach of Jantelagen.

One film scholar, for example, has suggested that legendary Swedish actress Greta Garbo—famous for her movie line "I want to be alone"—was not reclusive out of conceit but out of acute discomfort with self-promotion. "In my country, the papers talk about the King and Queen and royalty [or] otherwise about bad people," Garbo once said. "I do not want to have things printed about me because I am not one of any of these people" (Swenson 1997).

More recently, Swedish action movie star Dolph Lundgren, who has enjoyed some success in Hollywood, found himself the butt of jokes in his homeland when he appeared on a Swedish TV program and insisted on speaking English. Lundgren explained that he was preparing for a role in an American movie and trying to avoid the return of his Swedish accent, which would break his contract. But viewers rejected the explanation and accused Lundgren of believing himself "too good" to speak his own language. The fact that Lundgren had changed his name from the common Hans to the more exotic Dolph did not impress them either (even though their beloved Greta Garbo was once plain old Greta Gustafsson).

The Fear of Failure

Jantelagen also serves as a pernicious sort of defense mechanism. By not boasting or sticking your neck out, you avoid unnecessary risks, including the risk of failure.

A Swedish photographer recalled his father's reaction when he first showed interest in photography as a teenager. "My father refused to allow me to buy a high-quality camera," he related. "He said that photography 'wasn't something for me.'" It wasn't until one of his father's colleagues expressed approval of the idea (representing community acceptance) that the young man was permitted to pursue his goal. The story represents a personal example of a larger, societal problem, said the now-successful photographer. Looking back, he realized that his working-class father, representing the pre-World War II generation, was in some sense trying to protect him from disappointment or failure. But in the process, it taught him early in life not to take risks or to share his dreams. Even armed with this self-knowledge, he admitted to being cautious; he has found he keeps new ideas to himself until he is certain that they are realistic and can be accomplished without input or approval from others. (Note, however, that this is also an example of the Swede's need for independence.)

However, a new generation of Swedes, the Internet generation, is brushing Jantelagen aside. As we will discuss later in the chapter, the young entrepreneurs of Sweden's cutting-edge information technology (IT) and telecommunications industries don't consider Jantelagen a law that applies to them. They are successful, they are proud of it, and they are not shy about telling you about it.

The "Royal Swedish Envy"

One consequence of Jantelagen is what the Swedes themselves refer to as the *kungliga svenska avundsjukan*, or the "Royal Swedish Envy." It has nothing to do with royalty; the name is a reference to the fact that it seems as deeply rooted in Sweden as the monarchy or any other public institution.

Because of the value placed on absolute equality, there is a tendency to envy anyone who appears "too successful." In the United States, those who are very successful are often admired; in Sweden they are frequently criticized, which seems a logical consequence of living by the Law of Jante.

The American who sees someone else succeed says, "If he can do it, I can do it." The Swede says, "Who does she think *she* is?"

The following incident, reported in a feature article on Sweden in *National Geographic* (Belt 1993), illustrates how these attitudes emerge in response to attempts by individuals to excel. A Swedish engineer started his own company after being laid off from his job. Under the Swedish social system, he could have filed for unemployment and received a significant portion of his salary for a year, or he could have started a government job-retraining program to learn new skills. (This is common in Sweden, where many unemployed people take government-sponsored courses to "raise their knowledge level.") Instead of choosing either of these two options, the engineer decided to start his own home-based business.

One day, the engineer's next-door neighbor sprained an ankle, and the engineer's wife suggested she put a piece of meat on the sprain to stop the swelling. The neighbor's response was, "I guess people who have their own business can afford to waste meat! You must think you are something special."

But there is more behind the spirit of envy than Jantelagen. There may be a historical basis for these beliefs as well. In *Myterna om Svensken* (*Myths about the Swedes*), David Gaunt and Orvar Lofgren explain that nineteenth-century farmers were required to help neighbors who were less well-off, due in part to a belief in Luck, the very unpredictable whims of "Lady Fortuna." People believed that there was only a finite amount of Luck in life; for one man to become rich, another must become poor. Thus anyone who had good luck, made a lot of money, or had a good harvest shared his success with his less fortunate neighbors, for Luck is fickle and can be reversed (Gaunt and Lofgren 1984).

Strict parameters also governed how the fruits of one's success or luck could be displayed. Temperance in all things was encouraged, and displays of wealth, such as fancy clothes, were discouraged. That tendency continues today; a Swede told the story of an acquaintance who bought a new car, a brand-new Lexus sedan, with which to tour Europe with his wife. But he was embarrassed to drive it around the small town in Sweden where he lived; he didn't want the neighbors to find him ostentatious and talk about him behind his back. Envy wasn't just an emotion to fear in others; it was also to be avoided in oneself. Envy was regarded as a disease that one could easily catch; if you were the cause of envy, you could also "catch it" and become envious of others.

Envy, however, did not typically extend beyond one's own class; there was a marked (and accepted) difference between the nobility and the peasants. Only in the twentieth century did equality begin to be seen as more universal. Swedish ethnologist Åke Daun speculates that the growing income differentials now emerging in Sweden "will in the end bring about the weakening of the famous Swedish envy in that gaps between people will be considered part of the natural order: it is between equals that envy flourishes" (1996, 212).

Ironically, if a Swede were to win a large sum of money in a lottery, the reaction from his neighbors would now be more positive. Winning would be seen as a random, lucky event, which allows others to believe that they could be next. This may explain in part the Swedes' enormous appetite for lotteries and the like.

Jantelagen and Business

A Canadian American living in Stockholm made the following word associations with Jantelagen: "Non-excessive. Non-elitist. Give someone else a chance. Fairness." These are attributes that might be valued in many other cultures as well as in Sweden. But he went on to list others that are less positive: "Not my department. Lack of leadership. Promoting mediocrity." It is these latter potential attributes that have led many observers to see Jantelagen as a threat to Sweden's global competitiveness by potentially discouraging innovation. Jantelagen has not prevented Swedish businesses from succeeding, of course—modern multinationals from Volvo to SKF to telecommunications giant Ericsson offer ample evidence of success. While personally modest, Swedes are also early adopters and developers of new technology.

Interestingly, large corporations such as Ericsson and Volvo have found themselves to be somewhat immune to Jantelagen. Large corporations are permitted to succeed because they share their wealth (through taxes), provide jobs, and thus benefit many people. Entrepreneurs and small-business owners, on the other hand, are often seen as being in business only for themselves, and that creates envy. It is here Jantelagen may be most dangerous.

During the recession of the 1990s, some critics warned that the country's most creative period might already be behind it. "Our standard of living today is based upon a number of companies that were founded based on an invention made by a Swede 50 to 100 years ago," wrote Johan Ullman, a physician and inventor with the Swedish company Medinova, about multinationals such as Ericsson and SKF. Don't believe it? "Look at the stock exchange and think about it," he challenged (Dahlström 1997).

But what a difference a few years make. Sweden emerged from its recession to become the most IT-savvy nation in the world, in some reports surpassing the United States. The Stockholm region is being compared to Silicon Valley for its concentration of companies dealing in cellular telephony and telecommunications: they call it "Wireless Valley." Combine this with a comparable flood of Internet-related companies, and you must agree: Sweden is hot.

For those in their twenties and thirties, the IT generation, Jantelagen is somewhat of a relic. Like their American counterparts, they're bold, they're brash, and they're not afraid to take risks. "The information society and the new economy are driven by modern attitudes and values carried by the young generation," wrote Christer Sturmark, IT entrepreneur, author, and consultant (2000). This means it's acceptable to put your best foot forward when looking for that lucrative IT job. One young Swedish professional prefaced his online resumé with this tongue-in-cheek warning: "Jantelagen forbids Swedes from presenting their qualifications. The following is a crude violation of that law. Interested employers are invited to determine an appropriate penalty."

A young Swede working for a Stockholm-based public relations and Internet marketing company agreed. It is acceptable to state one's qualifications to obtain a job, but once employed, to continue to draw attention to oneself would mean "taking up too much space," he said, using a phrase that itself offers a serviceable definition of Jantelagen in daily life—don't take up too much space. That conflicts directly with the American tenet of making oneself visible on the job, standing apart from the crowd.

This is a difference that Swedes working with Americans already understand. To the traditional Swede, for whom anything that feels like an exaggeration is uncomfortable, the resumé tends to be a factual account of experiences and skills—that, the Swede believes, should suffice. As a result, a Swede's resumé may appear much less impressive than the resumé of an American with the same qualifications. The result could possibly be a missed opportunity. A Swedish manager working with Americans, conversely, is likely to be suspicious of resumés received from American applicants. One Swedish CEO said that he typically assumes the resumés he receives from Americans to be, on average, 30 percent inflated. Right or wrong, Swedish managers assume Americans exaggerate.

Are the Swedes next? Will high-tech success "turn the Swedes into flashy, greedy capitalists?" wondered a journalist with *Newsweek* International (McGuire 2000). "Sweden's 'show no chrome' philosophy runs deep," responded Paul

Saffo, a technology forecaster and director of the California-based Institute for the Future, in the article. "I don't expect to see Swedish dot-com CEOs riding around Stockholm in BMWs, Ferraris and Harleys any time soon." The young company directors may come to the office in jeans rather than business suits, he stated, but in many ways they remain "as restrained as their elders."

In fact, one of the biggest differences between Wireless Valley and Silicon Valley, Saffo added, is that "Swedes are very uncomfortable with new money, and especially conspicuous consumption." That would, of course, be quite anti-lagom as well as "anti-Jante."

The "Anti-Jante" Movement

Enjoying a thriving economy in the early years of a new century, many Swedes deny that Jantelagen still has a major influence on the country or its people. But others disagree. Not every Swedish company is a maverick, high-tech start-up. In general the effect of Jantelagen now seems most noticeable in areas where communities are smaller and more isolated.

Jantelagen thus remains an urgent national topic for Sweden because it continues to stifle creativity, according to John Steinberg, an American educator who has spent more than twenty years in Sweden. Steinberg was named "Anti-Jante of the Year" in 1997. The annual award is presented by Kairos Future, a Swedish company specializing in "future research," in recognition of efforts to combat the effects of Jantelagen. Steinberg won in part by doing the most anti-Jante thing imaginable: he nominated himself!

Steinberg has spoken to a number of Swedish groups on the dangers of Jantelagen. In an interview with one of the authors, he said, "The future is creativity. Previously, Sweden gained market share through quality," he noted, referring to the Swedes' tendency to let products "market themselves" based on their perceived high quality (in materials, design, production, etc.). "Now quality is a condition for being in the marketplace. Innovation is key. And how can you be an innovator if you're telling yourself and everyone else that you're not good enough?" In his talks he suggests setting rules for discussion that specifically shut down Jantelagen. "I tell them, 'Jantelagen doesn't exist in this room. Feel free to tell me what you think. Let your own ideas come out now.'"

Dismantling a cultural philosophy doesn't happen overnight. But in a true anti-Jante spirit, some Swedish consulting companies have found a niche in helping other companies break through the Jante barrier, Steinberg said. Jantelagen is becoming cultural shorthand for the old, the outmoded, and the negative. As a result, a number of "anti-Jantelagen" versions of the commandments have emerged, one of the most common being this variant:

You shall believe that you are someone.

You shall believe that you are as good as everyone else and everyone else is as good as you.

You shall believe that you are as smart as others, sometimes smarter.

You shall believe that you are as good as others—and if you know that you're doing your best, you can appreciate those that do it better.

Sometimes you know more than others.

You are not more important than others, but you are equally unique.

You are capable of a lot.

Laugh at yourself and your world—it will set you free.

You shall believe that many people care about you.

You shall believe that you can teach others much and learn from them as well.

Why? Because you are somebody—somebody who is needed.

The anti-Jante spirit has also been embraced at the community and municipal levels. In its strategic plan, posted on the Web, one northern Swedish community singles out Jantelagen as an enemy: "Our vision is to create a lively, dynamic region where the people believe in themselves and in the future, where Jantelagen is behind us and where it is [instead] fashionable to succeed."

Other communities have sought symbolic resolution. The northern town of Vittangi staged a mock trial of Jantelagen, sentenced it to death, and burned it at the stake—a seven-foot-high, hay-filled effigy of "Old Man Jante" went up in flames and with it, everyone hoped, Jantelagen's grip on Sweden. (In classic urban fashion, a newspaper columnist in the nation's capital responded archly, "Thou shalt not believe that we, in Stockholm, care about what thou doest up there in Norrland" [Ahlbeck 1998].)

In 2000 officials in the northern city of Sollefteå banished Jante by setting a Jante figure aboard a raft and pushing it out into the Ångerman River. "Jante appears in different disguises and represents an obstacle to positive initiatives," said Tomas Telje of Sollefteå's business development department in a press release. "That is why Jante is no longer welcome here."

And in the Norwegian city of Bergen, businesspeople pay good money to attend a seminar during which they cast stone tablets inscribed with Janteloven into the fjord. Divers wait under the water below the surface with new tablets bearing the tenets of *Vikingaloven,* or the Viking Law, an Anti-Jante variant that tells people "You are the best" and "You can do anything you want."

The Anti-Jante movement is well and good if not taken too far, according to Norwegian media specialist Borghild Gramstad, highlighting a beneficial side effect of Jantelagen/loven often overlooked. "When I hear about things like that, I think, 'No one is going to take Janteloven away from me.' Not because I have any desire to control the way others think, but because Jante also teaches us something else: namely, to have a healthy sense of skepticism about people who say they are better, know more, or want power over others," Gramstad wrote. "The essence of the positive side of Janteloven is the social democratic ideal that we strive toward here in Scandinavia: everyone shall have equal opportunities, everyone has equal worth, and no one shall unfairly rise up at the expense of others" (Gramstad 1997).

8

Equality above All

Ett lika fritt folk bör äga lika rätt.
(*A people of equal freedom should possess equal rights.*)
— Förenings- och Säkerhetsakten
(Sweden's Unity and Security Act, 1789)

Summary: Swedish policy makers have constructed a complex web of laws protecting the equal rights of Sweden's citizens and legislating equality between men and women, adults and children, Swedes and immigrants. Government-appointed ombudsmen speak up for underrepresented groups including the disabled, immigrants, and children. In 1969 Sweden officially endorsed and implemented a governmental policy of gender equality. Sweden has an unusually high proportion of women in the workplace, where unsupportable pay differentials are considered gender discrimination. Sweden's laws on equality have also made a far-reaching difference in family law, guaranteeing child care and enabling both men and women to combine jobs with parenthood.

The United States Constitution states that "all men are created equal." Swedes, too, are proud of the emphasis their country has placed on equality, the principle that every person has the same worth and value as every other person. It is,

97

in effect, the silver lining to the psychological cloud of the Law of Jante: you may not be better than anyone else, but you are certainly no less.

Whether Sweden's laws work adequately in reality is a matter of frequent debate; there is ample evidence that disparities still exist between women and men both in the workplace and at home. Cultural clashes with immigrants have also led to cases of discrimination and violence.

Nonetheless, Swedes do believe in the ideal and are willing to do what it takes to protect it. Equality is in some ways a "civil religion" for the Swedes, according to Harvard University's Brian Palmer. "One can see a 'civil religion' as a broad array of symbols and traditions that help us identify a collective identity, an interpretation of our common history, a feeling of a common goal to strive towards. In that sense, one can speak of a belief in equality as a civil religion among socially conscious Swedes" (2001). This religion may lack a deity, but it is no less morally compelling than any other religion.

Equality is the cornerstone of the Swedes' notions of independence and strength. While there is also admiration of the strong, there is great sympathy for the weak. Swedes place priority on establishing a minimum quality of life for everybody, whether weak or strong, and on minimizing differences between people. The financial means for doing so are taxes collected from the prosperous to distribute among those who are not. Laws protecting and paying for equality in Sweden represent lagom codified—no one should have more at the expense of others.

Democracy in Sweden is about more than the right to vote.* American democracy is based on the principle that the most just way to operate is by majority rule. Under Sweden's

---

* Incidentally, Sweden has one of the highest voter-turnout rates in the world, reaching the high eightieth percentile in the 1990s (*Statistics Sweden*, 2000).

social democracy, historically underrepresented groups such as women, children, the disabled, and immigrants receive more attention, not less. One way this happens is through the institution of the *ombudsman*—a concept that emerged in Sweden as early as 1809 and one of the few modern Swedish words to be incorporated directly into the English language. An ombudsman is a representative whose main objectives are to act as a spokesperson for individual citizens or groups in their contact with public authorities and institutions and to watch for any abuse of power. There are government-appointed ombudsmen in Sweden for the underrepresented groups mentioned in the previous paragraph, among others. Their duty is to listen to complaints from these groups, make sure that legitimate issues are handled properly, and educate the rest of society about the needs of these groups. The ombudsman represents an attempt to provide a balance of power and ensure the rights of those considered more vulnerable by society.

The sacred "Horatio Alger" myth tells Americans that the only thing standing between anyone and wealth is hard work and a little intelligence. There is a tacit belief that everyone "gets what he or she deserves"; thus, poverty is seen as a personal and moral failure. For the Swedes, poverty is viewed as a moral failure as well—but of society as a whole, not of the individual.

No One Is above Another

Striving for the ideal of a society without large class, gender, and economic differences has been a key component in the development of the Swedish Model. "Whether you are a waiter, bank clerk, janitor or finance director, people are treated the same," said an American woman living and working in Sweden. "No special treatment is given to those with money and it is highly looked down upon if you try to make a difference between the classes."

In 1809 the Swedish aristocracy deposed King Gustav IV Adolf, whom they considered incompetent, and installed a monarch of their own choosing: Jean-Baptiste Bernadotte, a French general who had served under Napoleon during Sweden's last war. Although technically the enemy, Bernadotte accepted the invitation and became King Charles XIV John; his descendents occupy Sweden's throne to this day.

His first act as king was to address the Swedish Parliament, the *Riksdag*, in Swedish, which he did—badly. The Swedes found his broken Swedish hilarious and roared with laughter. The stunned king was so upset that he never tried speaking Swedish again. Never had the Frenchman, product of an authoritarian culture, experienced subordinates who laughed at their superior (Hofstede 1991).

Quest for Gender Equality

The Swedish government has committed significant resources to addressing gender issues, with the aim of legislating gender equality into reality. One of the most important governmental positions is that of the equal-opportunities ombudsman, an independent government authority established under the Equal Opportunities Act. It provides information and advice to both employers and employees and acts on reports of sex discrimination in the workplace.

In 1969 Sweden officially endorsed and implemented a government policy of gender equality. One of its stated goals was to achieve an even distribution of power and influence between women and men, both on the individual and societal level. Other countries have announced similar philosophies, but few have followed through with Sweden's vigor.

To that end, legislation comparable to the U.S. Equal Rights Amendment and called the Act on Equality between Men and Women at Work, generally known as the Equal Opportunities Act, went into law in 1980 and was updated in

1992. The main purpose of the act is to promote equal rights for men and women with respect to employment, working conditions, and opportunities for personal development at work. The law not only prohibits sex-based discrimination but also makes substantial demands on employers to prevent it—and to prove they are doing so.

Swedish employers may not discriminate against a person because of gender. This applies to recruitment, terms of employment, direction of work, termination of employment, and job transfers. Employers are also required to take "active steps" to promote equality in the workplace. This includes preventing employees from being subjected to sexual harassment[†] and making it easier for both male and female employees to combine work and parenthood.

Pay differentials are also considered gender discrimination. It is illegal to pay a lower salary to one employee than to others of the opposite sex who perform the same job or work of equal value. Each year, employers with ten or more employees must conduct a survey of pay differentials between women and men at the workplace and analyze the results. The employer is required to draw up a plan of action to promote equality in the workplace. The survey and the measures that the employer plans to take to rectify disparities must be included in an annual report.

Despite the law, however, pay differentials persist between women and men. According to a recent study by Statistics Sweden, women's wages are on average 82 percent of men's. The study attributes much of the disparity to differences in the number of hours that women work, the kinds of jobs they choose, and the tasks they perform. But about five percent of the difference can still be attributed to discrimination, the study concluded.

Sweden has an unusually high proportion of women in the

[†] Sexual harassment is also illegal in Sweden, but lawsuits over incidents are much less common than in the United States.

workplace. This trend started in the 1970s, when economics made double incomes more of a necessity. In 1998 74 percent of women between twenty and sixty-four years of age worked outside the home compared with 79 percent of men. Women are much more likely than men to work part-time (27 percent versus 7 percent) because despite efforts to equalize male and female roles, women are still the main providers of child care and household maintenance.

Compared with the United States, where the prospect of a female president probably remains years away, Scandinavian women have made more headway in politics. Women hold key government positions and party leadership jobs in Sweden. Almost half of the Parliament members are women, and women are also well represented at the county and municipal government levels.

Women have had the right to vote in all elections since 1921. Sweden's largest political party, the Social Democrats, had both male and female candidates for high positions during its recent elections. In 1979, two years after the birth of Crown Princess Victoria, Sweden altered its law of royal succession, which was enacted after the abdication of Queen Kristina in the seventeenth century, to allow a woman to take the throne.

The great political breakthrough for women came in the 1994 election, during which women waged an aggressive campaign with the slogan "The whole salary—half the power." The intent was to show that there should, in fact, be equal pay and a real division of power.

In 1996, the government consisted of an equal number of men and women—eleven ministers of each gender—for the first time. Female ministers were responsible for foreign affairs, agriculture, justice, culture, labor, education, the environment, communications, social affairs, and equality affairs. Ten of the twenty-six undersecretaries for the state (the rank immediately below minister) elected that year were women. The Parliament Speaker was a woman. Altogether, 43 percent of the seats on the Parliament's standing committees, where most of the important political work gets done, were held by women. Despite all of this official gender-equality activity, however, men still dominate major policy-making bodies, critics point out. And in upper management of private industry, only about 10 percent of managers are women.

"In terms of being a woman and a leader, you can do anything you want in Sweden, as long as you don't rock the boat," according to Barbro Dahlbom-Hall, a Swedish lecturer and management consultant and author of *Leading Women: What Men Need to Know for Women to Grow.* "In other words, the real power has to stay where it's always been. But other than that, you can reach any position anywhere" (1999, 1).

Even in government, where women do hold a significant percentage of policy positions, "the boys are still in charge," Dahlbom-Hall said. "It is fine to elect a female foreign minister or a minister of education. But in reality, the 'three boys with their feet on their desks' are still dictating the rules and making the decisions."

This is also the case among senior executive positions within the private sector, she added, particularly in high-tech sectors such as telecommunications and information technology, where Swedish companies are among world leaders. In fact, Swedish businesswomen joke that the "IT" in information technology actually stands for *Inga Tjejer*—Swedish for "No Girls." This perception has now been shown to be fact: an investigation by the Stockholm daily newspaper *Dagens Nyheter* found that none of the twenty-two publicly listed IT companies could produce the annual action plan required by law to promote equality in the workplace.

Swedish feminists are right to point out that there is still much work to be done, noted Palmer. But despite lingering disparities in the private sector—particularly in senior management positions—Sweden is light years ahead of other nations in terms of women's empowerment. No other nation has as large a portion of women in the workforce, and "Sweden leads the developed world in the percentage of professional and technical workers who are women," he writes. He also references the American author Susan Faludi, who, after living in Sweden for some months, concluded that "if ever women are to take their rightful place in society, it seems likely that it will happen first in Sweden" (2000, 124–25).

The government's response, in true Swedish fashion, has been to study the problem; in 1993, for example, a commission was established to analyze reasons for the low number of women in top private-sector management positions. One result of this effort was the formation of the Business Leadership Academy, a group founded in 1995 to further knowledge, public debate, and efforts to increase the number of female executives in the private sector.

In 1994 the state appointed another commission to study the distribution of financial resources between men and women as well as the relationship between economic power and gender. Its aim was to investigate how economic policy affects the situation of both men and women, to make the difference in conditions for women and men visible, and to find ways to close the gaps.

"There still is some question of whether there truly is equality in the workplace when job ads say something like, 'Female between 25 and 40 needed to run the office as a secretary/receptionist/office manager,'" commented an American woman working in Sweden's technology sector. Several female managers work at her company, however, and she saw no discrimination on the job, she added.

Family-Friendly Policies

One area where laws on equality have made a far-reaching difference is family law. The aims of Swedish family law are to put women and men on an equal footing in marriage and to protect the financially weaker party in the event of divorce or death. The objective of related statutes, such as the Code of Parenthood and the Parental Leave Act, is to lay the foundations of shared responsibility for the home and children. Accessible child care has helped Swedish women make significant strides in the workplace, but the system was designed to benefit men as much as women, enabling both partners to combine jobs with parenthood.

Family-friendly parental-leave policies allow parents a total of twelve months off work after the birth of a baby, with one of those months reserved for the father. If the father elects not to take the month, it's lost, and the total leave drops to eleven months. The expectant mother can also take some time off in advance of the birth. The stay-at-home parent receives from 80 to 90 percent pay, and his or her job is guaranteed to be available upon return to work. Surveys show that more than 50 percent of fathers exercise their right to paid parental leave during the child's first year. When some men said that they were electing not to take time off because they couldn't afford the reduction in pay, some major Swedish companies, such as Ericsson, began an initiative to supplement the new fathers' income-replacement to reach 100 percent of their salary.

For toddlers and preschool children, Sweden guarantees accessible day care. This system evolved as more and more women started to enter the labor market in the early 1970s, explains Mona Danielsson, Sweden's assistant undersecretary for equality affairs. Twenty-five years ago, Swedish women faced the same situation many American women are facing today: more of them were working outside the home, but good child care was difficult to find. As a result, Swedish women began putting off motherhood, resulting in a birthrate that plummeted to near Depression-era levels in 1978. Policy makers realized that the country faced a future labor shortage—something that could reduce income-tax revenues enough to threaten the nation's social-benefit structure. The solution? Day-care and monetary incentives for women who have two or more children (although the latter program was terminated in 1996).

At that time future Parliament Speaker Birgitta Dahl had just been elected to the assembly. On the nights when sessions ran late, she had nowhere to send her children, and they ended up sitting in the hallway. She became a successful missionary for state-provided child care: at the end of the 1960s, there were only ten thousand day-care slots in Sweden; by the end of the 1970s, there were 130,000. Day-care centers may be municipally owned, run on a cooperative basis by parents or employees, or private—and there is one located right inside the Parliament building.

Today, day care is guaranteed by law for every child older than eighteen months. Child care is also available at after-school centers until children are ten. And how much do parents pay for public day care? About 10 percent of the cost.

Equality within the Family

Although women remain the primary providers of child care and household maintenance in many Swedish families, Swedish men and women share housework and child care to a greater extent than most American couples do. As mentioned in chapter 5, some immigrants to Sweden even ridicule Swedish men for their interest in cooking, baking, and staying home to care for the kids. Boys and girls are raised to see housework as something to be shared and working outside the home as valid for both men and women.

One Swedish woman described a cousin who is a stay-at-home Dad as a "gentle Viking." The six-foot, four-inch, broad-shouldered father of four works nights as a nurse and cares for the kids after school while his wife works outside the home. He cooks, cleans, and bakes bread (from scratch, she proudly points out) every week. And no one would even dream of calling him "Mr. Mom," she added. Once when one of the children was asked what his mother did at home, the boy thought for a moment and said, "She does the laundry." Children in Sweden are also considered individuals with rights that do not always coincide with those of the parents. Laws make illegal corporal punishment and any other form of punishment considered abusive, including hurtful language. Partly because of this, parents rarely discipline their children in public, and a public spanking would be nothing short of scandalous.

Most Swedish parents do not believe in a punitive form of child rearing; they prefer, as in other areas of their lives, to rely on reason. They tend to talk to their children more as they would to other adults. As a result, immigrants from conservative cultures tend to complain that Swedes have no control over their children and are inept as parents. In fact, many foreigners living in Sweden are used to a more traditional family structure, with an authoritarian father and very definite rules for children. This was the model in Sweden as well only a couple of generations ago; the situation only changed with the emergence of a system that specifically addresses the rights of children.

A Swedish social worker noted that, unfortunately, most immigrants have never been to a Swede's home. If they had, they would see that Swedes do discipline and teach their children, but in the privacy of their homes.

Equality and Relationships

When discussing "The Four S's" in chapter 3, we talked about the practicality with which Swedes approach the subject of sex. Equality plays a role in relationships also. Although Swedish women face the double standard regarding sex—including the notion that casual sex is acceptable for men but not for women—they encounter it to a lesser degree than do women in more conservative countries, including the United States. It is perfectly fine for a woman or a man to initiate a relationship, and they will most likely choose to split the check.

To women from other cultures, however, absolute equality can seem to produce behavior that seems, well, impolite. "You learn the Swedish definition of equality the first time you follow a Swede through a door and it swings back and hits you in the face," laughed an American woman in Sweden. "You don't realize how much you take for granted little things like men holding doors for you." Although many older Swedish men continue to hold doors, offer to carry heavy packages, or invite women to walk before them, the fact is that younger Swedish men are less likely to do so. Their behavior is not due to a lack of respect; it simply doesn't occur to them, but it can contribute to the perception by foreigners that Swedes are rude, when what is really at fault is a different perspective.

Many Swedish women, like many American women, resent any suggestion that they are incapable of performing basic tasks. Foreign men who customarily open doors for women in their own countries may find in Sweden the woman in question either flattered by the unexpected gesture or infuriated by some perceived suggestion of inferiority. It can be quite confusing. A young Swedish man working in the United States didn't understand, for instance, why a female colleague glared at him after he stepped into an elevator in front of her. An American co-worker later explained that American men often allow women to enter an elevator or pass through a doorway first. The Swede thought this ridiculous; to his way of thinking, the person who arrived at the elevator first should enter first. A Swedish woman would never want to be treated in such a patronizing way, he stated indignantly.

Similarly, the American woman who reported walking into doors tried explaining to skeptical Swedish colleagues that she was, in fact, a feminist. Such niceties are often performed in the United States out of courtesy, not chauvinism, she told them. Nonetheless, Swedish women and men alike belittled the notion as old-fashioned. That may not always be the case, however. When absolute equality means a lack of "gentle-manly" manners, some Swedish women would prefer a less-Swedish approach to day-to-day interaction between the sexes.

In "Where Are the Swedish Gentlemen?" writer Marie Hagberg in the Swedish women's magazine *Amelia* inter-viewed a Swedish college student and writer who suggested that it is time to open a finishing school for Swedish men. "They don't know how to flirt, they don't give compliments, they don't often bring flowers or presents, they don't open doors, and they only pay for themselves when you're out with them," she complained.

What about the vaunted Swedish equality? "We're not truly equal," she responded. "When women are really on the same footing as men [economically], then we can talk. Then it would be easier to accept their nonchalant behavior. But not until then."

A woman should still be allowed to be a woman, she went on. That means she sometimes wants to be treated "like a princess," she said. That is how an American boyfriend treats her. "He opens the car door for me, pays for us both [at dinner] and treats me like a real lady. He is also very atten-tive, something important that Swedish men miss."

In other words, sex roles in Sweden can be just as confus-ing as they are in the United States or in any other Western country. The key is to remember that the Swedish ideal is for men and women, adults and children, Swedes and non-Swedes, and managers and employees to have equal footing in life.

9

The Seasons and Their Power: Summer, Winter, and Holiday Swedes

It is as if one had been tied up in a sack, and someone cautiously undid the top, making a sunny blue slit...At this point people go slightly mad, they clear away the snow drifts and turn their pale winter faces to the sky. If you see, anywhere on Earth, someone peering hungrily at the sun, you can be sure that he is a Swede.
  —*Sweden: A Year*, Lena Larsson

Summary: As a result of the dramatic differences between the seasons in Sweden, the "Summer Swede" and "Winter Swede" appear to be totally unlike each other. The lack of light in winter has a depressant effect on many, while the abundant light of summer energizes all. Many Swedes enjoy a special relationship to nature, and through cycles of plant and animal life, they track the progress of the seasons. Holidays, too, represent important milestones; the Swedes seem to live from holiday to holiday. And because summer is so short and so valued, the Swedes insist on their right to vacation time to enjoy it.

> The returning seasons, so much more noticeable by the extremity of their contrasts and their swift replacement of each other, give rise to a heart-touching poetry such as one would have to be made of iron not to feel.

These are the words of Paul Britten Austin in *On Being Swedish* (1968, 126). He is right: in few places do the effects of the seasons so strongly affect both the mood and behavior of a people as they do in Sweden and other areas of the far north. There is a remarkable difference between the "Summer Swede" and the "Winter Swede," and no one is any more aware of this than the Swedes themselves.

Sweden's seasons are very distinct. The winter is long and dark; the spring, short and often wet; the summer—what everyone has been waiting for—comfortable, with long days and delightful evenings that seem to last forever; and the autumn, vibrant with color but marked by shortening afternoons that bear witness to the approach of winter.

The Swedes' sensitivity to the seasons is related not so much to changes in temperature but to the varying amount of daylight, a result of the ever-elusive (and completely unreliable) sunshine of any given season. The temperature in Sweden actually averages eight degrees centigrade warmer than that of other countries at the same latitude because of its proximity to the warm Atlantic Gulf Stream (Kisthinios 1996). By the end of December, however, the days are very short, and the far north sees almost no daylight at all. Stockholm remains dark until 9:00 A.M., and evening begins to fall by 3:00 P.M. Of course, by the end of June, northern Sweden is bathed in light twenty-four hours a day (hence the nickname "Land of the Midnight Sun"), and night in Stockholm is very brief.

As a result of limited sunlight, some Swedes (and others elsewhere, for that matter) experience a type of depression called Seasonal Affective Disorder during the winter. Thanks to new awareness of this syndrome, however, many people now seek ways to compensate for the lack of sunshine, such as special light screens that simulate sunlight. Light screens have even been installed in a few Stockholm cafes, allowing people to enjoy a cup of coffee and some much-needed light therapy at the same time. However, one of the most popular (and traditional) ways for Swedes to get a "sunshine fix" remains heading to warmer climates during the winter months, making charter tours to southern Europe and Florida a thriving business.

Not every Swede flees the country during the winter, of course. Outdoor activities, including skiing and snowmobiling, are incredibly popular. For others, winter is a time to slow down, recharge, and do things they don't otherwise have time for, such as catch up on their reading.

The Signs of Nature

The wax and wane of sunlight is just one way the Swedes track the progress of the seasons, particularly winter into spring. For many, the cycles of nature are just as important.

Many Swedes recognize the arrival of spring through the return of the migratory birds—the larks and cranes—and a succession of flowers. The first garden flowers of the season, the *snödroppe* (snowdrop) and *krokus*, emerge while snow is still on the ground. In the woods hikers look for the first *tussilago* (coltsfoot), *blåsippa* (hepatica), *vitsippa* (wood anemone), *gullviva* (cowslip), and, finally, as the weather warms toward the end of May, *liljekonvalj* (lily of the valley). With the arrival of summer comes nature's bounty: wild strawberries and blueberries, tart red lingonberries, and, as autumn approaches, wild chanterelle mushrooms.

What foreign visitors may find astonishing is that heading out into the woods, basket in hand, to gather flowers and pick berries and mushrooms is somewhat of a national pastime in Sweden. Many Swedes find great pleasure in the quiet and solitude of the forest, which represents a welcome respite from a hectic day-to-day lifestyle. The Swedes, who seem to be so nonreligious (or "postreligious" as some may call them) may nevertheless be so reverent of nature that they experience something akin to spirituality in this relationship. A Swedish woman who had lived abroad for many years recounted a visit with a fellow Swedish expatriate. When the conversation turned to the topic of nature, she shared her feeling of awe when taking a walk by a lake in midwinter, struck by the beauty created by the sun's reflection on the ice. The man responded with a story of his own. He had invited some English friends for a tour in his sailboat to show them what he considered an amazingly beautiful part of Sweden's western coast, a region characterized by rocky islands and sparse vegetation. Swedes find the coastline's stark beauty inspiring. As they sailed by the area the Swede found so beautiful, however, all his guests could say was, "When do we get there?" They did not see what he found so special. This deep appreciation of nature must be something very Swedish, he concluded.

Beauty is in the eye of the beholder, of course, even natural beauty, and there is something profound about the Swedish appreciation of nature. A longtime resident of Sweden, originally from Chile, said that after more than fifteen years, he was beginning to feel a peculiar appreciation for the beauty of nature. Walking along the coast with his family one day, he watched a flock of birds arise from the water and burst out, "That is so beautiful it hurts!" It struck him then that perhaps he had become more Swedish.

One reason for the Swedes' connection with nature and the outdoors may be *Allemansrätten* (every man's right), a general right to public access that is unique to Sweden. This ancient law guarantees every person access to any woodland or wilderness, even land that is privately owned. The law supposedly originated from the concept that all people should be allowed the opportunity to provide for themselves in order to survive. Today, it means that Swedish natural areas are for everyone to enjoy. You can, for example, go for a walk, have a picnic, camp, or pick flowers (assuming they are not a protected species) and berries or mushrooms for your own use (that is, not to sell or replant) in the forest without worrying about being chased away or arrested.

But with freedom comes responsibility. Visitors are expected to "leave no trace" of their presence; this means not damaging or littering the landscape, packing out one's trash, and keeping a respectful distance from the homes of others and not disturbing their privacy. It certainly does not mean one can trespass in someone's garden or orchard to pick their fruit, as some tourists have mistakenly believed. Unfortunately, the fact that Allemansrätten is sometimes abused by foreign visitors has led to resentment on the part of the Swedes.

Because of their love of nature, Swedes are some of the most environmentally active people in the world. They are avid recyclers, they do not allow or appreciate excessive packaging materials, and they have strong restrictions on chemicals used in cleaning products. Even expired medications are returned to pharmacies for proper disposal. Business decisions in Sweden are likely to take the environment into consideration to a much greater degree than occurs in the United States.

During the 1990s Stockholm hosted an annual event, the Stockholm Water Festival, in mid-August. This week-long affair, held in the center of town, commemorated the success of Sweden's own water-reclamation activities. Once quite polluted, the waters surrounding the fourteen islands of the Swedish capital are now pure enough to support healthy salmon, and fishers angle from downtown bridges. It's even safe to go for a swim. The festival culminated with the awarding of the Stockholm Water Prize, presented by King Carl XVI Gustav, to a company or group that made a special effort to improve or prevent further damage to the earth's water supply anywhere in the world. The award continues to be bestowed each year.

Winter Traditions

Highlighting the natural seasons on the Swedes' annual calendar are the major holiday seasons. It often seems as if the
Swedes live from holiday to holiday.

When fall arrives and the days begin to shorten, the Swedes
disappear into their winter coats, hurry home from work, and
seem to hibernate. Spending all this time indoors, families
and couples make a special effort to make everything cozy
and warm, or *mysigt*. This is part of the Swedes' love of
stämning, a concept that is a bit difficult to translate. The
closest equivalent in English may be "creating an atmosphere." But the Swedish word also carries strong emotional
overtones of closeness and togetherness.

One of the most popular ways of creating stämning is by
lighting candles. Swedes are fond of candles, particularly
during the dark winter months, and one of the most popular
holidays in Sweden features candles in abundance: St. Lucia,
on December 13.

Swedes have celebrated December 13 as a holiday for centuries, but not always for the same reason and certainly not
in the same way. At the winter solstice, thought to be the
longest and darkest night of the year, hobgoblins and witches
were said to walk the earth and do things like kidnap naughty
children. As recently as a few generations ago, men took to
the streets in blackface and costumes to make mischief on
Lucia Eve; this custom has disappeared, but some teenagers
have taken up partying and causing trouble as part of "seeing
Lucia in."

In the Middle Ages, the pre-Christmas fast began on Lucia
Day. People were not allowed to eat meat, only fish, until
Christmas. By the time Lucia Day came around, the autumn
work was supposed to be finished. Among other things, farmers were supposed to have stored all their grain and slaugh-
tered and prepared whatever animals were to provide the
Christmas delicacies.

On the eve of Lucia Day, both man and beast were to get a little extra something— a "Lucia bit." The animals each got an extra sheaf of oats or some tidbit from the kitchen. When morning came, it was the family's turn, and everyone feasted at breakfast before the fast began. The tradition of celebrating December 13 with a Lucia procession (*Luciatåg*) is more recent. Dressed in white, wearing a crown of candles, and surrounded by a procession of white-clad attendants St. Lucia makes her appearance all over town. As the participants move along, they sing what has become the traditional Lucia song—Swedish verses describing the magical appearance of St. Lucia, set to the Italian melody of the same name.

Families reenact their own Lucia rituals at home: a young girl dressed in a long, white Lucia gown, joined by her brothers and sisters, serves her parents coffee, *pepparkakor* (gingersnaps), and *lussekatter* (saffron buns) in bed, extremely early in the morning on the thirteenth.

Lucia Day as it is celebrated today commemorates St. Lucia of Syracuse, a Catholic saint. Lucia was born in Italy in the third century, at the height of the Roman Empire. Many legends surround her courage in the face of persecution as a Christian, but all of them end with her execution on December 13, 304, and her later canonization.

In one story Lucia was promised to a man who was not a Christian. Women traditionally brought a dowry with them when they wed: money, livestock, or expensive gifts. But Lucia gave away her dowry to poor Christians. When her fiancé informed the Romans of Lucia's deed, they tried to execute her. First they tried to drown her—she survived. Then they tried to burn her to death—again she survived. Finally, they ran her through with their swords—and this time she died, her white gown soaked by her blood. This is why present-day Lucias have a red ribbon tied around their waists.

According to another story, Lucia was a Christian girl with beautiful eyes. A prince fell in love with her, but because he was not a Christian, Lucia refused him. To demonstrate her faith in God, she popped out her eyes and gave them to the prince, whereupon he immediately converted to Christianity. Lucia's eyes were then restored by the Virgin Mary, which is why Lucia is said to be the patron saint of vision. The name "Lucia" has also been connected with the Latin word for light, *lux*.

Viking traders who became Christians supposedly brought the legend of St. Lucia back to Sweden. During a time of terrible famine in the Middle Ages, a large, white vessel loaded with food and clothing appeared on Lake Vänern in south-central Sweden, and at the helm stood a beautiful maiden in a gleaming white robe, her head encircled by a crown of radiant beams. As soon as the ship was unloaded, it vanished. The grateful people believed that the maiden who had come to save them was St. Lucia.

Today, Swedish schools and towns have their own Lucia processions, and Stockholm even holds a national Miss Lucia pageant each year. Because Lucia Day falls at the time when Nobel Prize-winners are gathered in Stockholm to receive their awards, it has become a tradition for Sweden's Miss Lucia to awaken the Nobel Prize-winners in the wee hours of the morning with the traditional coffee and saffron buns. Some startled recipients have compared the predawn experience to hallucinating the appearance of an angel.

An American orchestra conductor who has now spent many years in Sweden shared the story of his first St. Lucia observance. He had been on the job for only a couple of weeks when a number of his colleagues decided to surprise him by appearing at his home early on the morning of December 13, singing the Lucia carol and bearing saffron buns. He groggily answered the door and, neither being familiar with the tradition nor recognizing his new colleagues, assumed the people were trying to sell him something! "No, thank you," he said, closed the door, and went back to bed. He arrived at work later that morning with a lot of apologizing to do.

Jul (Christmas) is celebrated in Sweden on December 24. Long before the Christian celebration of Christmas became a traditional holiday, pagan Swedes celebrated the "midwinter feast" (Kisthinios 1996). Christmas in Sweden is quite secularized today, but many people who don't normally attend church do so for *julottan*, the worship service that is held very early Christmas morning. It is an event of wonderful stämning, where the church may be lit almost entirely by candles.

Santa Claus, called *Jultomten*, arrives on the afternoon or evening of Christmas Eve, not through the chimney when everyone is asleep but in person through the front door, to the delight of small children. (A family member or friend dresses up to do the honors.) The Christmas dinner consists of a big smorgasbord featuring an array of traditional dishes. Unlike in the United States, in Sweden Christmas dinner tends to be very similar from household to household. The mainstay is a baked, cured ham; other staples include meatballs, *lutfisk* (an infamous fish dish consisting of dried cod that has been soaked in lye and then boiled), and rice porridge. Preparation for this event begins early in December, including much baking of both bread and cookies. Swedes still prepare a great deal of food from scratch, bake bread regularly, can berries, and prepare and freeze mushrooms.

In December visitors are welcomed in from the cold with a cup of *glögg*, a hot, spiced, red wine drink that may or may not be fortified with spirits of a more transparent variety. Guests help themselves to a spoonful of raisins and sliced almonds, and heart-shaped pepparkakor are served with the drink.

Unlike in the United States, where the day after Christmas is just another shopping day or workday, in Sweden the day after Christmas is also a holiday and another day off work. This means that depending on what day of the week Christmas falls, there is likely to be little work done between Christmas and New Year. In fact it can be quite a while after the New Year before business is back to normal, because

January 6 is another holiday, and Christmas is not officially over until January 13. Businesspeople are advised to plan accordingly.

The Rebirth of Spring

As spring approaches, the Swedes celebrate Easter, which marks not only the death and resurrection of Christ but the pagan rebirth of spring as well. An important Easter decoration is a bouquet of birch branches decorated with colorful feathers. The branches, immersed in water, soon begin to sprout pale green leaves, an early reminder of the springtime greenery soon to come. Legend has it that people once used the birch branches to whip each other as a reminder of the suffering of Christ, but don't try this one on your new Swedish friends!

Easter, like many other holidays in Sweden, retains hints of more superstitious times. On the day before Easter, little girls dress up as witches with painted faces (in this age of equality, little boys now can dress up in costumes as well). Wearing their mothers' long skirts and scarves tied under the chin, they go with a coffeepot to knock on their neighbors' doors, expecting to receive a coin or piece of candy (in exchange for a hand-decorated Easter card, in some regions). This tradition originated in the superstition that evil spirits were at work at this time of year, represented by witches who flew on broomsticks to the Blue Mountain to conspire with the devil. The witches are appeased with a small gift.

On Easter Eve, a special dinner is served, incorporating egg dishes. Boiled eggs are decorated by both adults and children. Instead of an Easter egg hunt, children receive fancy paper or plastic eggs filled with candy.

The last day of April is *Valborg*, or Walpurgis Night, a major celebration all over Sweden, particularly in university towns. Bonfires are lit in the evening, and people gather 'round to drink and sing songs about nature, springtime, and the blessed summer—often shivering in the very unsummer-like evening chill as they do so. Traditionally, adults don their high school graduation caps (white caps with black visors, not mortarboards), a tradition that dates back to a time when only a very small portion of the population graduated from high school.

High school graduation in itself is a festive event in Sweden. Family and friends wait for the graduates to storm out of the school and greet them with flowers and plastic toys to be hung around their necks as well as with ridiculous signs aimed at embarrassing them a bit. After the students are properly congratulated and "decorated," they and their well-wishers sing the traditional "Student's Hymn," a tune penned by a Swedish prince and known by all. Then they may be transported home for a party on some kind of unusual vehicle—ranging from pickup trucks to fire trucks—decked out in birch leaves and balloons.

The last day of the school year is special for younger students, too. The children gather in the assembly hall or in a church (one of the few times you will actually find a lot of Swedes in a church), and once again, as part of the ceremony, they sing songs and hymns about nature. There is probably not a Swede alive who hasn't felt slightly emotional upon hearing the words of the most well-known hymn, "*Den blomstertid nu kommer*" ("The time of flowers is now coming"). The song is an ode to the beauty and freedom of the summer season to come.

Finally: It's Summer!

In June watch out: the Summer Swede emerges! Everyone and everything moves outdoors. Any opportunity to serve coffee or a meal out in the backyard or on the balcony is seized. On Friday afternoons everyone is struggling to get out of the office and head for the country. Many Swedes have a *sommarstuga*, or summer cottage, where they can escape from the city. Here, they retreat to fish, sail, or just relax. Yet it often seems that the Swedes never work harder than when they are on vacation; there's always gardening or work to do on the cottage, and the sounds of hammers and chain saws resonate throughout the land.

Those who don't own a place in the country may rent a garden plot outside the city center. These plots allow people without access to a garden to grow their own vegetables and flowers—a way to "be in the country" in the city. These so-called "garden colonies" began in Stockholm in the early 1900s as a way for people who had moved in from the country to escape to something a little more like home.*

The major summer holiday on the Swedish calendar is Midsummer. Celebrated the weekend nearest the summer solstice, Midsummer was originally a pagan and agrarian event. Now, however, it is the year's biggest party. By the time it arrives, the Swedes have truly emerged from their winter doldrums and are ready to celebrate the joys of summer.

Midsummer is the ultimate celebration of nature. The centerpiece is the maypole, originally an ancient, pagan fertility symbol. Maypoles can be found, large or small, in all parts of the country and are raised in public parks as well as on private properties. Adults and children gather in a ring around the maypole and dance—to the accompaniment of traditional accordion and fiddle music, if they're lucky. These dances, also referred to as "dance games," are familiar to anyone raised in Sweden and can be quite amusing to watch. It's not every day one has the opportunity to observe adults jumping around, pretending to be little frogs! Could these Swedes be the same people as those bundled-up beings rushing home in the winter darkness without looking at anyone?

---

* These little patches still make quaint places to visit, as many feature dollhouse-size cottages and are bedecked with fruit, vegetables, and flowers.

In August comes the final, very Swedish celebration of summer: the *kräftskiva*, or crawfish party. In the United States crawfish are generally associated with Louisiana and Cajun cuisine; they are eaten during those months of the year when it is considered safe to eat shellfish. In Sweden, on the other hand, crawfish are eaten only during a short period in August because, traditionally, crawfish harvesting was restricted in order to preserve the supply. Today, most crawfish eaten in Sweden are imported, many from Louisiana, where they are prepared Swedish-style—boiled in salted water with a crown of dill and other special seasonings—before shipping. The kräftskiva is sometimes referred to as a kid's party for grown-ups. This is a pretty good description for an event where everyone sits at long tables dressed in funny crawfish hats, wearing paper crawfish bibs, singing drinking songs, and frequently behaving like a bunch of rowdy kids! The guests noisily devour their boiled crawfish, slurping their salty brine, stopping only to butter their bread. For many a foreigner this can be quite an exotic experience, especially for those who have only encountered the reserved, sometimes shy Swede in other social situations. The crawfish party, where the aquavit flows freely and a shot of the clear liquid is chased with a mouthful of beer, brings out quite another side of the Swede.

A similar party takes place later in the month for the annual debut of another fishy dish: *surströmming*, "sour, fermented herring." This pungent-smelling dish is decidedly an acquired taste, however, and its popularity is limited primarily to northern Sweden.

A warning to the uninitiated guest participating at a crawfish or surströmming party for the first time: aquavit with a beer chaser should not be taken lightly. Crawfish parties are renowned for more drinking than eating—it takes too many crawfish to counteract the effect of the "water of life." Many a foreign visitor not aware of the potency of this potion, eager to keep up with his or her Swedish host, has ended up in a stupor with a serious headache the next day. A final caution:

Sweden has very strict drunk-driving laws; prior arrangements for a ride home are imperative.

The Sanctity of Semester (Vacation)

As we have seen, by the time summer arrives, the Swedes are ready to take advantage of every opportunity to squeeze all they can out of this brief but wonderful season. The summer months are almost holy in Sweden. The weather is a topic of constant conversation and consternation, as rain is a frequent, uninvited guest.

In the United States, you earn your vacation time; in Sweden, you have a right to vacation. Swedes by law receive five weeks of *semester* (vacation), and most take it during the *industrisemestern*, or industry vacation time, in July. Many Swedish businesses slow down at this time, and some companies shut down completely. Even those who must work are likely to try to get away whenever they can. When the weather is warm, employees will also likely leave work early, especially on Fridays. It is not a good idea to schedule important meetings on Friday afternoons during the summer.

For foreign colleagues, this long slow period can be difficult to cope with, especially if they are trying to move projects forward, make decisions, or meet deadlines. To make things even more stressful, much of the rest of Europe vacations in August, which can cause additional headaches for anyone trying to coordinate European business activities this time of year.

Times are changing somewhat with increased globalization. Multinational companies and others that rely directly on the global economy are changing their work habits and vacation schedules, but it will be hard to get the Swedes to give up any of their precious semester. They must, after all, store up on sunshine for the long, dark winter to come.

10

Communication: The Sound of Silence

"Tala är silver, tiga är guld."
(To speak is silver; to remain silent is gold.)

—a Swedish proverb

Summary: Silence in conversation often makes Americans nervous; they will do anything to avoid it and say anything to fill it. In Sweden, however, silence is a trait to be valued. Swedes are generally uncomfortable with small talk, finding it unnecessary or, worse, intrusive. Instead, they see conversation as something that should have a purpose. When they do communicate, however, they can be surprisingly blunt. This is due to the fact that Swedish is a very direct language and that Swedes tend not to sugarcoat information. While they willingly participate in serious conversations and insist on truthfulness, they tend to dislike conflict and will often retreat from confrontational encounters.

Even when people speak the same language in the same country, cultural issues can emerge. So we shouldn't be surprised when we find it challenging to understand and be understood abroad (even in a country like Sweden, where

125

most people speak some English); yet we almost always are. We feel frustrated when others do not share our style of conversation or respond to our efforts to communicate in ways that we recognize. Communicating means connecting with others, and this is one of the greatest challenges when meeting anyone from another culture. As human beings, we communicate through spoken language (the words we choose and how we say them), through body language, and through our actions.

When it comes to communicating with others, Sweden has been described as a land of voluntary introverts. This chapter's opening, a time-honored Swedish expression, advises that "to speak is silver; to remain silent is gold." Even Swedes who don't consider themselves shy may seem reserved by American standards. Famous Swedes are often noted for their silence: Greta Garbo, skier Ingemar Stenmark, and tennis players Björn Borg and Stefan Edberg come to mind. Even Sweden's national anthem refers to the country as "you ancient, you free, you mountainous North; you *silent*, you joyous beauty...."

Chapter 5 noted a connection between the Swedes' reserve and their sense of privacy. A conversation is a way of inviting someone into your world. Some people, however, feel uncomfortable about letting others get too close, at least initially. Others ascribe this character trait to the Swedish sense of melancholy. A 1990 article in the satirical U.S. magazine *Spy* offered faux phrases to "help" travelers to foreign nations. Some phrases listed for Sweden included "Look at all the concrete!" (a jab at Stockholm's depressing, 1960s-era suburbs) and "How skillful you are at hiding your inner angst!" (a reference to the legendary emotional storm beneath the cool Swedish calm).

But more plausible reasons for the Swedes' silence are much simpler: their reluctance to "take up too much space" combined with an admitted dislike for and inability to engage in small talk. The fact that they refer to it as *kallprat* (cold talk) and *dödprat* (dead talk) offers some insight into the dread they have of social conversation. If the Swede can't be *duktig*—good, proficient, and certainly not foolish-looking— he or she doesn't want to say anything at all.

While Americans are brought up to say nothing if they can't say anything nice, Swedes are brought up to say nothing if they have nothing important to say, positive or negative. In many Western countries, including the United States, silence often makes people nervous. Confronted with an awkward pause, an American tends to insert small talk, jokes, or questions to keep the ball rolling. Swedes may find this aimless conversation superficial or even tiresome. The more you talk, the longer they listen—and the quieter they become.

For the Swede conversation should have a purpose, particularly in a business context, explained Bengt Andersson in his *Swedishness* (1993). One converses to "increase one's knowledge of something, explain one's position on a certain issue, or confirm an agreement" (88).

Swedes are not fond of small talk. They don't understand why Americans they have just met ask them personal questions, such as whether they are married or have children. What they don't realize is that the Americans have a wallet full of photos, and they are just dying to be asked about their families themselves.

One of the authors offers in her consulting practice "lessons" in small talk for Swedes. "There is often a pattern to the art of good small talk," she tells them. "If you listen, you may begin to see that it often involves a progression of questions, such as 'Where are you from?' 'Where did you go to school?' and 'Where do you work?' These kinds of questions allow two people who have just met to find some common ground, which is important in a country like the United States, with such an incredible mix of people from diverse backgrounds."

Small talk is not, she warns, the place for serious or controversial questions such as "Why do Americans believe in the death penalty?" There is a time and place for those types of conversations, but small talk is not one of them. She offers suggestions for Americans as well: "If a Swede lapses into a long period of silence, take a deep breath and try not to force the conversation. He or she is likely contemplating what was just said or thinking through what to say next." And while a Swede may find questions about his family to be rather personal when meeting someone new, asking about his professional specialty or favorite hobby can be a good conversation starter. Also, the Swedes are also almost as good as the Brits when it comes to discussing the weather!

Of course, everything is relative. To the Finns, for example, the Swedes seem downright gregarious, and there are enormous regional differences as well. The further north in Sweden one travels, the more reserved people tend to become. A Website for a northern Swedish beer poked fun at this well-known characteristic with its "simple rules of thumb for conversation" in the north—but they could apply anywhere in Sweden:

1. *Kallprata inte.* Don't make small talk. You don't need to talk to pass the time.
2. Don't brag.
3. Don't "suck up" to people.
4. Don't yell.
5. Just relax.

Fairly introverted Americans may even find themselves an extrovert in the eyes of their Swedish colleagues. In fact sometimes Swedes seem to expect Americans and people of other more gregarious cultures to take the lead or break the ice in social situations. This can be disconcerting for Americans who happen to be shy. At company events "People kept looking at me like they expected me to do something," said an American woman who, ironically, is Swedish American and considers herself rather reserved.

Silence Is Golden

Confronted with the archetypal quiet Swedes, some non-Swedes come away with the impression that Swedes are bored, indifferent, or even rude. Their silence, however, does not mean that something is wrong, even though it is sometimes difficult to know just what their quiet demeanor does mean, author Herman Lindqvist noted (on a return trip to Sweden after having lived abroad):

> My first morning in Sweden was an experience. I ate breakfast at the hotel. There were 20 people in the dining room. It was absolutely silent. The only sound to be heard was that of cereal being chewed. No one said anything. No one looked at anyone. Just that chewing, and the rustle of the morning newspaper.... I learned that in Sweden, there isn't just distance between automobiles and homes. There is distance between people as well, in this land of evasive glances and enormous silence. (1989, 223)

Asked to explain, a Swede would probably say that the silence Lindqvist wrote of most likely reflected not unfriendliness but regard for others' privacy and comfort—no one wished to disturb another's breakfast with meaningless and distracting conversation. This plays to the Swedes' desire to leave and be left alone, unless invited. To an outsider, however, the silence could be disconcerting.

Non-Swedes sometimes take silence to mean tacit approval. This is not necessarily the case either, however. An American communications director recalled her first meeting with the Swedish company that had bought her American firm. She shared her interpretation of the company's recent employee survey while the assembled company of Swedish managers listened silently, nodding occasionally. She assumed they agreed with her conclusions; it turned out that they were simply being polite.

"I thought when they nodded, it meant 'Yes, I agree,' when it actually meant 'Yes, I understand,'" she said. (In this respect the Swedes are much like the Japanese, with whom they are often compared in certain aspects of cultural characteristics.) To understand their thinking and gain their input, the American communications director discovered she had to ask them questions. "Ask them directly, 'Is this what you think we should be doing?' Then they will tell you, but unless you ask, they won't always give you the feedback you need!"

Similarly, she found that when she sent Scandinavian managers e-mail, she would get nothing back, as if the Internet were "a black hole." The problem, she learned, was that she wasn't asking the right questions.

The Swede will usually present a request in a very straightforward manner, at least in his or her eyes. A seemingly nondirective comment such as "We need to have this done by Friday" means "Do this by Friday." The statement "I'd like for us to get it in the mail tomorrow afternoon" means "Get this in the mail tomorrow." In both cases the Swede finds the request polite, empowering, and very clear because there is a specified time frame attached. But it is a firm time frame. If asked to do something that you may not be able to deliver, do not, for example, say yes, expecting to come up with a reason to postpone when the deadline arrives. If you doubt you can complete the project, it is best to say so right away. Swedes who work with Americans commonly complain that the latter make commitments they will not be able to keep. Americans in business are conditioned to respond with 100 percent certainty, because anything less may suggest they are less than competent. Thus, they can find it difficult to say "No, we can't do that" or "I'm not sure I can do it by then," when that is precisely what the Swede wants to hear, if that is the case. For the Swedes' part, they need to understand that Americans do not do this out of dishonesty, but to avoid an uncomfortable situation.

Likewise, if you want a Swede to do something, be very

specific. Avoid expressions such as "as soon as possible." If you specify a date or time, a Swede will feel obligated to complete your requested task without excuses. By asking for a response by a specific time, the American communications director found her Swedish colleagues responded promptly and either met her deadline or beat it.

Keep in mind that writing a letter in a foreign language is not easy. Someone who finds it intimidating to read and then respond in English may postpone answering any correspondence. Once again, this is often due to the fact that the Swede feels uncertain about "doing it right," being duktig. What if she doesn't use the correct form of address or the proper closing or makes grammatical mistakes? This may be enough to cause her to put the letter at the bottom of the pile and wait to hear from you again.

Fortunately, e-mail seems to work much better. First, the Swedes are among the most "wired" people in the world and comfortable with high-tech communication. Second, the rules for composing e-mail are more relaxed and less likely to be a source of worry, although, like other forms of Swedish communication, their e-mails are likely to be very brief. Another alternative is to correspond by fax and request that comments and approvals be noted on the fax and returned. This method also eliminates the need to compose formal letters.

Nonverbal Communication

Swedish women don't seem to have the same difficulties communicating or expressing themselves, at least not to the degree that some Swedish men do. This could be due to the greater freedom that women in most Western cultures have to show their emotions and reach out to others (although Swedish women may smile less than, say, American women).

In general, the Swedes' nonverbal cues—such as body language and proxemics (their need for "personal space")—are like those of North Americans and Australians. That is, they look directly at conversation partners while speaking and listening. They usually leave two to four feet of space when talking to an acquaintance or stranger and are not likely to touch during conversation. There is, however, other nonverbal behavior to watch for. For example, many Swedes have a tendency to listen with a very "closed" and sometimes intimidating posture: folded arms held in front of the body, back stiff. They believe they are demonstrating their seriousness, but it doesn't encourage open or comfortable communication. Similarly, very direct and prolonged eye contact is a way of demonstrating attentiveness. It can be disconcerting for an American speaker to look out at a sea of stony faces. He may make a number of faulty assumptions—that the participants lack expertise, are bored, or even agree with him—all while the Swedes are just showing respect for the presenter.

Non-Swedish presenters are sometimes dismayed when they reach the time set aside for questions and answers and encounter only silence. Yet after the presentation, they may be approached by a number of individuals with questions. Here the Swedes' reluctance to stand out and make fools of themselves comes into play. Americans don't hesitate to state their opinions in front of others; it can be an opportunity to shine. Swedes, with their typical caution, may not only be afraid of appearing foolish in front of a group but may also feel that it is impolite to cut in, particularly if the situation calls for correcting another person's statement. (If that is the case, Swedes are more likely to approach the speaker afterward for a one-on-one chat.) If you plan to conclude your presentation with a question-and-answer period, it might be wise to arrange with someone in the audience to ask the first question and break the ice.

Swedes are also much less likely to walk around with smiles on their faces than are many Americans. To smile for no real reason is to be false, according to the Swede, who thus thinks that people who smile too much are superficial or lack self-control. Many Swedes, particularly men, do not betray very much emotion in their facial expression. A composed, serious face, though, can lead to the misimpression that one is angry, unhappy, unfriendly, or even arrogant, especially when combined with long periods of silence.* One of the authors often counsels Swedes in the United States to try to smile a bit more—not encouraging them to be false, but to be aware that it makes Americans more comfortable.

Blunt Talk

The inverse of the Swedes' silence is bluntness. When you do ask a Swede for her opinion, she will most likely give it, with no sugarcoating. That is, if a Swede disagrees with you, he will do so calmly but without the polite prefacing seen in other countries, such as "I see your point, but..." or "That's an interesting view, but...." This directness can be perceived by some Americans, particularly women, as rude; women are often taught that it is polite to "be nice" and to minimize disagreements.

Act that way in Sweden, however, and you risk "coming off as a politician," said a Swedish scientist living in the United States. His manner of directly contradicting colleagues with whom he disagreed earned him an initial reputation as being arrogant, he admitted. Eventually, his American boss took him aside to explain that his way of communicating offended people. Because he was so blunt, his colleagues had taken his criticism personally, although that was not his

---

* Nowhere, perhaps, is this more evident than the world of politics. Whereas an American politician is expected to play the hail-fellow-well-met, the Swedish politician is unlikely to laugh and slap backs with the same gusto. To do so would be seen as forced and false; instead, the Swede is more likely to present a somber and serious persona that may be interpreted as intelligent, arrogant, or dull, depending on one's point of view.

intention. In fact, most Swedes are generally reluctant to criticize other individuals—unless they are politicians, public officials, or "overpaid" leaders of large corporations. Some of this bluntness can be traced to linguistic differences. Swedish itself is a "muscular" language without a lot of polite embellishment. For example, it features numerous ways to say "thank you," but no single word for "please." (This unusual ratio actually reflects an important aspect of Swedish character brought up earlier in the book: no one wants to be a bother, but expressing gratitude is important.) Combined with an absence of pleasantries or small talk, a simple request can sound terse to foreign ears. Keep in mind that it is difficult when speaking a foreign language to grasp all of its nuances and to know when one is coming across as curt or abrupt.

Because they tend to be forthright, Swedes often take the words of others at absolute face value as well, which can occasionally lead to misunderstandings. For example, the managers of a Swedish telecommunications company were baffled to learn that the American they had brought over to visit their headquarters did not enjoy his stay in Sweden. During his two weeks there, he hadn't mentioned any problems, yet upon his return, it was obvious that he clearly was not happy. He told co-workers he felt his Swedish hosts had ignored him.

The Swedes, upon hearing this, did not understand. They had asked him if he wanted to get together outside of work, but he had replied that he was "fine." The Swedes, interpreting what he said literally, did not insist; they assumed that either he preferred to be alone or had other plans. The American, on the other hand, had expected them to insist on entertaining him. His initial response had simply been one of typical American "politeness"; he did not want to appear pushy, but he obviously had had certain expectations.

In this situation the American wasn't untruthful or the Swedes unfriendly; they merely interpreted each other's messages using their own communication protocols. "Had [the American] said 'I'm fine, but if you would like to do something, I'd be glad to come along,' the outcome would likely have been different," said a Swede in reaction to hearing about the American's discomfort.

Conversely, many Swedes new to the United States have suffered hurt feelings or at least confusion because of comments by Americans such as "How are you doing?" or "Let's get together for lunch." Swedes (as well as other foreigners) tend to take these statements literally and will give a truthful answer to the first and wait for an invitation (or make one themselves) following the second. If their response that they have a head cold is met with a blank stare, or if the lunch invitation never comes, Swedes may judge American behavior as insincere or superficial. They don't understand that these phrases are often used simply to convey friendliness in the U.S.; the Swedes are simply not accustomed to saying things merely to be nice (even if they are nice!).

Retreat from Conflict

Although Swedes insist on truthfulness, they typically dislike heated confrontations, preferring to avoid conflict when possible. They often interpret excessive emotion as a lack of control or immaturity and, when faced with it, will retreat into silence, if not into another room. A Swede who disagrees with you is more likely to just walk away than engage in a heated discussion. Yelling—particularly in a business setting—is simply not lagom.

Swedish management expert Lena Zander points out that the Swedes' conflict-avoidance preference also has a rational aspect: "There is a strong belief that conflict is ineffective and will hamper the process rather than energize" (1998, 4).

In cultures where public displays of emotion are more acceptable, conversations often become quite loud. For the Swede raised voices imply either lack of control over one's emotions or a substitute for logically and rationally proving one's point. Loudness in social situations annoys Swedes, and they interpret it not only as bad manners but also as evidence of a conflict, which makes them uncomfortable.

In the Swedish daily newspaper *Svenska Dagbladet*, a group of Italian immigrants recalled their impressions of Sweden when they first arrived as guest workers after World War II. The Italians were being escorted by an Italian-speaking Swede, who noted with apprehension the increasing volume of the Italians' conversation in the train's dining car. He waited for an appropriate moment to make a statement, then delivered with considerable humility the following:

> Because I know your country and your temperament rather well after living abroad for many years, I will take the liberty of giving you some well-intended advice. There are [Swedish] passengers who want to come in here for something to eat, but when they hear such loud voices, they have to stop and wonder. They think there's a fight going on.

The Italians then realized that they really were coming to a country that was not their own and to a people who were different: they were loud, the Swedes, quiet. Would there be other differences, they wondered.

There are occasions, however, when the Swedes can be anything *but* quiet; their voices definitely become raised after they've raised a glass or two or when they are in a group (or often both). As discussed in chapter 3, "The Four S's," alcohol functions effectively as a social lubricant in Sweden; it is all right to let down your guard when drinking. This mirrors the behavior of the Japanese, who use social drinking after hours as a safe way to voice opinions that they dare not offer at work.

The same Swede who didn't make a sound during your entire presentation this morning is now telling corny jokes and asking women whom he doesn't know to dance—something he may surprise you by doing rather well. What strikes you even before he starts chatting away is how his body language has changed: His arms are no longer folded in front of him. He is smiling. He turns out to be a charming dinner partner. This is the "inner Swede," finally released from the confines of lagom and Jantelagen and liberated from the fear of committing some embarrassing faux pas.

Similarly, a group of Swedish soccer or hockey fans have no qualms about painting their faces blue and yellow and hollering—if they're all doing it—just like a group of rowdy American football fans. An individual Swede, however, unless put up to a stunt by his friends, is unlikely to put on a solo show.

Natural Language

Most Swedes are likely to speak very good English, thanks to years of schooling and English-language entertainment. (Unlike countries such as France and Germany, which dub over TV programs and films, the Scandinavian countries use subtitles.) Even so, it is important to remember that English is still a foreign language and that it can be tiring to speak any foreign language for long periods of time. For this reason, Swedes will frequently begin speaking Swedish to one another, even with non-Swedish speakers present.

An American executive working for a major Swedish telecommunications corporation in the United States reports that his Swedish colleagues—who tend to socialize only with one another—are known around the company as the "Swedish Mafia." Many Americans and other foreigners are struck by this separatism and may find it frustrating or threatening. They feel excluded and may believe that the Swedes are talking about them.

Generally, however, Swedes don't speak Swedish to exclude others but because it feels more natural to speak their own language with another Swede. Often they do it to exchange information quickly and efficiently, particularly if they believe the subject at hand to be of no interest to anyone else. They may be surprised to learn that this offends others. In fact, Swedes do not always include even other Swedes in conversation. A Swedish woman living in the United States had met a Swedish friend for lunch when a colleague of his stopped by to say hello. The colleagues began discussing a business-related topic, and neither made any effort to include her; her friend didn't even bother to introduce her. Because she had lived in the U.S. for many years, this behavior felt somewhat strange to her—most Americans would offer at least a perfunctory introduction. But under the circumstances, the colleagues believed that their relationship and topic of conversation were "strictly business" between them and probably of no interest to her. This also demonstrates how the Swedes often separate work and private life.

Many Swedes find it awkward to walk up to and introduce themselves to strangers. Like many of us, they prefer to talk to people they already know and often talk to the same person throughout a social event. Also, as we have noted, they can be quite lax about introducing people who join the group to the others present.

An American who wanted to do his part in breaking the Swedish habit of staying in one "safe" place a whole evening made special arrangements when asked to organize a social gathering. He told the hotel manager to remove all the chairs from the room where the event was to take place. When they asked why, he explained that removing the chairs would make it more difficult for the Swedes to "park" themselves in one location for the entire evening! He hoped this would force them to talk to more people—and it apparently worked.

A word on humor: it rarely translates well between cultures. Americans' penchant for sarcasm, in particular, often puzzles the Swedes. Making fun of others is less popular in Sweden than in the United States, and people who do so are perceived as being mean-spirited, causing Swedes discomfort.

One American man said his Swedish wife hates programs like *Candid Camera*, for instance, because they embarrass people. The Swedish sense of humor tends to be rather dry, and jokes are often told with a completely straight face. As a result, foreigners often believe that the Swedes have no sense of humor. To the Swede, who has brought down the house at a number of dinner parties, such comments are difficult to understand.

Building Social Competence

"Swedish society is trying to become more extroverted, more outwardly oriented," explained a Swedish freelance journalist. "Swedes are suddenly realizing that this is a characteristic that is very valuable in the global economy." Increasingly, he noted, Swedish employment ads seek individuals with not only the professional qualifications for a position but "social competence" as well, a concept loosely defined as the ability to get along with and communicate well with others.

The move toward developing social skills is also in part a response to Sweden's increased international visibility as part of the EU. Swedish television programs have criticized Swedish politicians for their inability to make themselves understood in English at international meetings and for their wooden appearance on camera.

Swedes see themselves as practical people, and even in an area as subjective as communication styles, if there's a problem, they want to solve it—rationally and systematically. As we mentioned early in the book, the Swedes are avid pursuers of education and not shy about participating in organizations, including groups such as Toastmasters, which can help them develop their public-speaking ability in English and in Swedish. (Ericsson and Volvo are among the businesses where employees have started chapters.)

The Swede has often been compared to a bottle of ketchup. You pound and pound with no results—and then, when he or she feels comfortable enough to open up, suddenly the ketchup comes gushing out. When interacting with Swedes one-on-one, it is often simply a matter of gentle persistence to reach the "inner Swede," the person who wants very much to talk with you.

11

Manners: Swedish Customs Simplified

STOCKHOLM, Sweden—As it moves into Sweden's far north, McDonald's is minding its manners by offering diners knives and forks for eating hamburgers. The chain had several outlets in northern Sweden in 1987–91 but didn't offer utensils even though local custom calls for their use.

"We were a little rigid and held tightly to our concept, but now we're listening more to what our customers want," Kjell-Arne Forsberg, an executive for McDonald's in Sweden, was quoted as saying to the Swedish news agency TT.

The outlets that closed in 1991 were taken over by the Max AB chain, which offered knives and forks. "It certainly wasn't that that decided the competition between us, but for many customers it was a significant difference," Max marketing manager Hans Söderqvist told TT.

—Associated Press, November 17, 1997

Summary: Customs are notorious for being cultural minefields. Behavior that is considered polite in one culture may be completely unacceptable in another, and telling the difference is often something that occurs only in hindsight. Outsiders are surprised to find that the same Swedes who eschew titles are annoyed by guests who don't arrive exactly on time

141

or, worse yet, arrive on their first visit empty-handed. And then there is the mysterious Rule of Shoes....

In order to distinguish the polite from the impolite in Sweden, especially from the casual American perspective, one must understand recent changes in the country's social history. Sweden is today a much more informal country than it was just fifty years ago, a country where it was once taboo not only to use someone's given name but even to refer to him or her directly as "you." Swedish, like French, Spanish, and German, has both a familiar and a formal form of the pronoun *you*. However, prior to World War II, it was common for people to go to great lengths to avoid using either of them, which would involve making an uncomfortable judgment regarding personal familiarity. Instead, they resorted to addressing each other in the third person: "Would Dr. Andersson [or simply "the doctor"] care for some coffee?" "If it is no trouble for Mrs. Olsson."

Today, nearly everyone uses the familiar pronoun *du* for "you." Employing the formal *ni* between Swedes may actually be interpreted by some as insulting, as it implies distance or even condescension. (Not to worry, though, foreigners attempting to speak Swedish tend to be universally forgiven all faux pas.) Most adults, both men and women, introduce themselves with a handshake and first and last names. They expect to be called by their first name. Titles are seldom used, even the courtesy titles of "Mr." and "Mrs." that are still commonly used in the United States and absolutely essential in other European countries such as Germany and France.

For Americans, this first-name protocol can feel deceptively comfortable, but beware; it simply reflects the Swede's egalitarianism and doesn't necessarily translate to the familiarity or intimacy an American might assume.

Coming from children, the use of first names can be disconcerting. Most Americans are still brought up to address adults as "Mr." or "Mrs." unless invited to do otherwise.

Swedish students call even their schoolteachers by first name. Only the most elderly relatives are addressed as "Aunt" or "Uncle," and even that is disappearing.

Many American children are also raised to the mantra of "please" and "thank you." As previously noted, Swedish is a language with many ways to say "thank you" and no true equivalent to the word *please*. Instead, Swedes use phrases such as "be so kind and..." or simply add *tack* (thank you) to a request, as in "Shut the door, thanks." Thus, when speaking English, "please" may not automatically spring to the Swedish mind. When speaking with a foreigner in English, the request may come out simply as "Shut the door," a request (command) that may sound somewhat rude to American ears.

The Rule of Shoes

Every country seems to have special rules that apply only to it. So if you remember nothing else before trotting off to Sweden, warns David Curle, "remember the Rule of Shoes." In an interview with one of the authors, Curle, an American writer and IT specialist who lived in Stockholm for several years, identifies one of the most common mysteries of Swedish manners: to remove or not to remove your shoes when entering someone else's home.

On his Swedish-American Website titled "KulturChock!" Curle adopted the tongue-in-cheek role of *Etikett-Professorn*— the Etiquette Professor—to answer questions about Swedish manners and etiquette, starting with footwear. It is customary for Swedes to remove their shoes when entering the house, theirs or anyone else's, customary but not absolute.

For those who want to begin their journey toward social acceptance in Sweden, the Etikett-Professorn offers the one tip most likely to have a positive effect: the Rule of Shoes. The Rule of Shoes is very simple, Curle asserts wryly: "Never, ever wear shoes inside another person's home. Unless, of course, others are doing so."

It is easy to see where this practice originated. From the Swede's point of view, removing one's footwear upon coming inside makes sense; it keeps the floor and carpeting clean, especially during the wet winter months. That doesn't mean that Swedes always walk around in socks, however. Most keep a pair of "inside shoes" handy at home for slipping on after the "outside shoes" come off. Because this seems so sensible to the practical-minded Swede, the notion that people in other countries don't remove their shoes can come as somewhat of a shock.

What he or she cannot explain, however, is why, even in Sweden, it is impossible to predict when or where the Rule of Shoes will be broken. Curle shares an experience of his own. He is invited to a party at a colleague's home in Stockholm along with co-workers and several of the firm's clients. When he arrives, he notices that everyone is dressed to the nines. "After about five minutes, however, I realize that among all of these nicely clad people, there is not a single pair of shoes to be found!" He looks down at his loafers and, red with embarrassment, excuses himself to use the bathroom. "I sneak down the hall to place my shoes among the many lined up in the hallway, which I should have noticed on the way in."

Same location, one year later; many of the same people are in attendance, but this party is slightly less formal. He greets his hosts at the door and confidently pries off his loafers. He walks into a room full of smiling colleagues and feels curiously short. The reason, of course, is that everyone but him is wearing shoes.

"Ask a Swede about this—when you wear your shoes and when you take them off—and he will give you a look as if you had just asked him how he breathes or why he drinks a snaps," Curle says. "He does not know; he just does it. The only recourse for those of us not born and bred with the Swedes' innate shoe sense is to simply do what everyone else is doing."

His advice? "Look your host directly in the eye, shake his hand, then look down at everyone's feet. Do not leave the entrance hall before ensuring that your feet are in the same state of dress or undress as everyone else's."

Managing Social Occasions

The Rule of Shoes is a humorous example of some of the pitfalls of socializing in a new country. The Swedes, though, take their dinner parties seriously. Inviting someone into one's home is a major step for the reserved Swedes, and they will go to great lengths to ensure a well-executed evening of good food, the right wine, and interesting company. Punctuality is a virtue in Sweden. When it comes to entertaining, there is no such thing as "fashionably late." Americans joke about the Swedish penchant for walking around the block rather than ringing the doorbell at 6:55 P.M. rather than 7:00 P.M. Nonetheless, an invitation for 7:00 P.M. means 7:00 P.M. Those who arrive early feel they are inconveniencing their hosts; those who arrive late will be red-faced to find the evening has started without them. Similarly, anyone appearing late for a business meeting, for example, had better have a good reason. Keeping people waiting as a way of demonstrating power not only will not work but is likely to backfire: no one is above buying and using a watch.

One interesting exception to this is *akademiska kvarten*, or "the academic quarter (hour)." This tradition started (and continues) at Sweden's University of Uppsala, where classes typically do not begin until fifteen minutes after their listed starting times. The reason? Students hundreds of years ago had no clocks or watches to tell the time. Church bells ringing on the hour alerted students to the start of class; they then had fifteen minutes to appear. Today, businesspeople may joke that someone who is late is working on akademiska kvarten. After fifteen minutes have passed, however, he or she had better have a good explanation for being late.

It is customary to present the host or hostess with a small gift such as a box of chocolates, a small plant, or flowers the first time (or even the second time if it has been a long time between visits) you are invited over. This is common practice even among young people. (The correct way to present a bouquet of flowers in Sweden, incidentally, is with the paper wrapping removed. Cellophane can be left on.)

Another area that often trips up non-Swedes is attire. The dress code in Sweden is in effect the reverse of the prevailing one in the U.S. Until the recent advent of "business casual," Americans dressed up for work and often dressed down when going out socially. The Swedes, except for those in more conservative companies such as banks, do the opposite. They tend to dress very informally at work. Long before casual days hit the U.S., it was not unheard-of to see a Swedish man dressed in sandals (with socks), jeans, and a short-sleeved shirt, not always well matched. But when invited to dinner at someone's house, guests are expected to be well turned out, with a jacket or a fashionable dress.

Even Swedes who should know better find this habit hard to break. To celebrate the Fourth of July in 1998, newly named U.S. ambassador to Sweden Lyndon Olson decided to share something from his home state of Texas with the Swedes and host a real Texas barbecue. The invitation stated "casual dress." But this did not prevent several Swedish gentlemen from arriving in coat and tie—including the chief of protocol from Sweden's foreign department! Meanwhile, Ambassador Olson enjoyed himself in his short-sleeved polo shirt and slacks. When a Swede issues the invitation, however, it is safer to overdress than to underdress, unless the invitation is to one's summer cottage or boat during the summer.

The Honor of Toasting

One of the most time-honored of Swedish customs is the toast. From a formal dinner to a simple social evening with friends, it is likely that the evening will include a toast. In fact proper protocol states that you should not touch your drink until the host has made a welcome toast. When you toast in Sweden, raise your glass, make eye contact with the other people at the table, nod slightly, and say *skål*, which means "cheers," before taking a sip. Then raise your glass again and briefly make eye contact again with the others before setting the glass down.

Do not, as many Americans do, clink glasses. That is not the Swedish custom, and it is likely to precipitate an awkward round of uncomfortable clinking among confused guests.

At a typical dinner party, the guest of honor is seated to the left of the hostess (or host, if there is no hostess). This position typically bestows upon the occupant the duty of making a few clever and, hopefully, amusing remarks. Should you be called upon to say a few words—the phrase in Swedish is *hålla tal*—don't worry about making a major speech. Custom calls for the speaker to simply stand and thank the hosts for inviting him or her to the event and for the pleasure of their company and that of the other guests. Then lift your glass first to the hosts and then to the other guests at the table in a toast.

A word of explanation about the tradition of seating is also in order. Couples, unless just engaged, are not typically seated together. Instead, guests are matched as table partners to encourage people to mingle and meet one another. When dinner is served, the gentleman in the pair escorts his partner to the table. (On a related note, should there be dancing after dinner, don't be surprised when Swedish men ask married ladies—that is, other men's wives—to dance. This is not only acceptable, but considered polite and sociable.)

Once seated, eating the European way, with fork in left hand and knife in right, is considered the correct way. Most Europeans have had enough contact with Americans to know that they have a different way of wielding a knife and fork. Still, some older Swedes may interpret a fork in the right hand as less-than-perfect manners. And as the epigraph illustrated, in some areas of Sweden, eating without a knife and fork is simply impolite, even for hamburgers or pizza.

After dinner, thanking the host and hostess for the meal before leaving the table is imperative. In other cultures, it might seem strange and even a little abrupt to say *Tack för maten*, literally, "Thank you for the food," but showing thanks shows good manners in Sweden. Similarly, it is customary to thank the hosts after the event is over (*tack för senast*), either by phone or the next time you meet them.

Time for More Coffee

Swedes are among the world's leading consumers of coffee, and the beverage plays an important social role. Traditionally, meeting for coffee has been a social ritual. A foreigner's first invitation from a Swede is likely to be to meet for coffee. Visitors to Sweden can expect to be served a lot of it at many occasions—but not until after the meal. Americans' habit of drinking coffee with their dinners confounds Scandinavians in general.

When Sweden was still a patriarchal society, the men would gather after dinner (Swedes still enjoy a cup of coffee after dinner, but company is now mixed) for a *kaffekask*, a cup of strong coffee fortified with a shot of something a bit stronger. Today, a nice dinner is usually followed by a cup of coffee and a brandy or other drink. Many Swedish companies take a *fika*, or coffee break, at 3:00, and some also take one in the morning at 9:30 or 10:00. The coffee break in Sweden is an important social gathering, a time to talk about what one is working on or doing. Management and employees sit together and drink coffee and eat cookies, sweet rolls, or cake, and not showing up is considered impolite.

One American working for a small company in southern Sweden found the ritual midafternoon break difficult to get used to, especially since she didn't care for coffee. With typical punctuality, the Swedes would begin calling her name at three o'clock to drag her away from her desk. "And they made fun of me because I brought tea bags!" she reported.

Birthdays also represent grounds, so to speak, for an office fika. In an interesting twist, however, individuals celebrating birthdays are typically expected to provide the birthday cake, often a *princesstårta* (princess cake), a fancy layered confection of vanilla and raspberry covered with a green marzipan icing—a combination that tastes much better than it sounds. In part because of the high cost of alcohol, many Swedes are more likely to meet at a local cafe, or *konditori*, to have a fika rather than to visit a bar or pub. Having people come to one's home for coffee is also a tradition. Many a Swedish household has a freezer full of homemade cinnamon rolls or cookies ready to be quickly thawed and served to the drop-in guest. In fact, an advertisement for Gevalia, a famous Swedish coffee brand, touts its high-quality product as perfect for just that "unexpected visitor."

This coffee culture has led the Swedes, like many other Europeans, to consider themselves coffee connoisseurs. Many a Swede visiting the United States has commented on the sad state of standard American coffee: "This isn't coffee; it's just dirty water," as one Swede put it. "I can actually see the bottom of the cup!" Fortunately, the current coffee-house revolution taking place in the U.S. has made it easier for Swedes to find coffee "worth drinking." But don't be surprised if you find that Swedish companies in the U.S. import their own coffee from home.

The Clean Plate Club

The American popular habit of taking home leftovers in a "doggie bag" has not caught on in Sweden, except perhaps in some pizza restaurants. It is not quite the norm. Nor is it as much of an issue, given that food portions in Sweden tend to be significantly smaller than those served in the United States. Over the last few years, however, some restaurants have embraced the American trend toward larger portions, lagom or not.

There is, however, one Swedish dining experience that seems to defy the concept of lagom, and that is the famous smorgasbord. Don't, however, think of the smorgasbord as an American buffet, a free-for-all where one can load up on a multitude of dishes at once. No, there are rules for how to eat from a smorgasbord; books have been written on the topic. Here is the short version. Begin with a sampling of the cold seafood dishes, such as pickled herring. Once finished with that course, take a clean, new plate and move on to the cold cuts. Repeat the process with the hot dishes such as meatballs and Jansson's Temptation, a casserole made of potatoes, cream, onions and anchovies that is considered by many the national dish. Finally, finish the feast with dessert and coffee. And don't load up on more than you can eat. It is considered poor manners to leave too much food on your plate when you are finished eating.

12

Doing Business in Sweden: Competition versus Consensus

Consensus is more than simple agreement—it means that everyone buys into the decision you make.

—a Swedish company president
working in the United States

Summary: Differences in how Swedes and Americans do business fall under four main categories: competition, decision making, corporate structure, and communication. Because individual competition has a negative connotation in Sweden and consensus is not always a top priority in the United States, these are areas of potential misunderstanding in the mixed workplace. The Swedish and American planning styles also differ considerably, with Americans taking action much more quickly than the cautious Swedes. These characteristics have also led to the evolution of a flat management structure and informal communication style among Swedes that can be as challenging for Americans to adapt to as it is for Swedes to deviate from.

If imitation truly is the sincerest form of flattery, the Swedes can feel flattered by the fact that many aspects of their business management style are emulated in other countries, including the United States. Project-management theory in the U.S. now stresses the importance of longer planning periods and increasingly emphasizes the role of team building.

At the same time, some areas of Swedish management practice could benefit from exposure to the American model. The Swedes might find themselves even more successful in today's supercharged global economy by embracing more flexibility and a quicker decision-making process.

Because of its small population and relative geographic isolation, Sweden has long been forced to look beyond its borders for business opportunities. Perhaps because Sweden has a long history in commerce—one could say that it stretches all the way back to the Vikings—the Swedes consider themselves well versed in the ways of international business. The industrial and engineering firms of the early twentieth century required access to a market larger than Scandinavia in order to succeed, and they led Sweden's modern charge abroad. Today, Swedish products are used around the world.

Yet many foreign businesspeople, including Americans, can find it unexpectedly frustrating to do business with the worldly Swedes. Once again, because of the relatively minimal language barrier, both Americans and Swedes often assume that they approach business in a similar manner. This, however, is not necessarily the case.

> The funny thing was, if you put two project managers together, one American and one Swede, the first time they met, they'd say, "This guy is super! This will work out perfectly!" Well, six months down the road, the problems would start, and a year down the road, they would be enemies,

said Magnus Moliteus, former president of Swedish-owned pharmaceutical company Pharmacia USA, in an interview with one of the authors. A resident of the United States for some twenty years—and now a naturalized U.S. citizen—

Moliteus is former director of the U.S. office of the Swedish government's Invest in Sweden Agency.

The problems could stem from any of a number of factors, he says (including some of the personal communication issues taken up in chapter 10), but if the workers survived that rough initial period and made it past the two-year mark, they came to an understanding. "They might not understand each other fully, but they could appreciate the differences."

Beyond their differing styles of communicating, the two cultures approach doing business in fundamentally different ways. With a basic understanding of the Swedish cultural patterns already covered in this book, however, including independence, lagom, Jantelagen, and equality, these differences indeed become easier to appreciate—and maybe even to understand.

Noncompetitive Spirit

The subtitle of this chapter, "Competition versus Consensus," would seem to imply that these two concepts are mutually exclusive and cannot coexist. That, of course, is not quite the case; however, the Swedes do have a greater desire to reach consensus (i.e., be inclusive, work together toward a common goal) than to "be the best." The relationship between the two approaches to business merits further investigation.

When describing values inherent in American culture, competitiveness holds its own among those such as freedom and independence. Competition in the United States is considered both a positive and a necessary force. It reflects the national value placed on personal achievement and striving to be number one: first, fastest, biggest, best. In Sweden, by comparison, competition, at least on the individual level, is frequently regarded with some ambivalence. Furthermore, it is not a major thread of the social fabric, in a culture where legislated equality and personal moderation are dominant values.

Unlike American children, who grow up in a society that encourages healthy competition with peers from an early age, Swedish children are not raised in a highly competitive environment. They are taught not to play up individual abilities. As discussed in chapter 8, showing off or boasting is likely to be met with disapproval. Today, schools do not even give grades to younger children. In an attempt to foster individual development, children are encouraged to do only their personal best. This tends to decrease the competition among students and keeps the environment from becoming what Swedes perceive to be excessively competitive. Instead, teamwork and cooperation are posited as the best way to reach a common goal.

As we have discussed throughout this book, Swedes learn many of the prerequisites for successful teamwork during childhood. Former American ambassador to Sweden Lyndon Olson recalled a scenario he encountered not long after arriving in Sweden. It was a cold winter day in Stockholm, and he was riding in his car when he noticed an unusual sight and asked his driver to stop. He had spotted a preschool class out for a walk, the children all bundled up in brightly colored snowsuits. But what had caught his attention was the fact that the children were connected in a line with a rope. Where one went, so did the others. This was obviously done to keep the children safe during the outing. What made such an impression on Olson was that he saw this as an example of how the Swedes learn from an early age to work together and not against one another.

Although Swedes, like all people, do enjoy their personal achievements, they tend not to bask too long in the glory of an accomplishment for fear of being perceived as boastful. This has the effect of decreasing competition except in situations where it is considered positive, such as sports or business, where an individual represents a larger entity such as a sports team, company, or country.

"If it means people look primarily to their own well-being or that of their own department, then competition could be perceived as a negative," commented a Swedish manager at the U.S. headquarters of a Swedish multinational company. "Internal competition may produce better performances overall, but if you focus too much on the individual level, you can lose sight of how the team is doing."

These limits are not necessarily imposed on the individual, however; some Swedes shun direct competition to avoid being singled out for responsibility. "Living through such successes is 'safe,' " was the harsh judgment of a Swedish scientist who has chosen to make his home in the United States. "There is no personal disaster if the team lost, your company did poorly, or the country failed in a sport.... It is a form of shirking individual accountability that most Swedes wouldn't even recognize in themselves."

Competition at Work

In an example of how differently two people can view the same situation in terms of competitiveness, Moliteus tells the story of a Swedish manager and an American manager who decided to play golf as a way of getting to know each other better:

The weather was terribly unpleasant; it was raining cats and dogs. After six holes, the Swede said, "Hey, this isn't so great—should we stop?" And the American thought to himself, I'm the new guy on the block. Is he testing me, to see if I'm strong enough? So the American responded, "No, we should go at least nine holes." The Swede didn't dare say no. Later, I asked him whether he knew the American felt tested. "No," said the Swede. "I was soaking wet and tired and I wanted to go back to the club and have a beer!" He didn't realize that the American took it totally differently.

The Swede, not raised in as competitive an environment, is more likely to take an interaction at face value—and to call a spade a spade when necessary. The American, on the other hand, more often looks for the message between the lines, in this case reading into the situation a competitive challenge.

According to Swedish ethnologist Åke Daun, "Part of the Swedish mentality is a readiness to compromise, which in Sweden is considered a prerequisite for civilized relations between people with conflicting interests" (1996, 155). This attitude makes it natural for the Swede to embrace consensus, and it helps explain the reluctance to be "too competitive." Competition assumes an ability to accept differences and to value that which stands out—neither of which is readily appreciated in Sweden.

An example of how the Swedes' low-key attitude toward competitiveness may hurt them in business is in the area of marketing. A Swedish company known in Europe and less competitive markets may underestimate the enormity and competitiveness of the U.S. market, where visibility is key. It is essential that a company differentiate itself from competitors, no matter what the quality of its products or services. Without substantial investments in marketing and advertising, chances are a company will find it difficult to be successful in the United States. But this kind of aggressive promotion is a major leap for some Swedish companies to make—quality, they believe, should speak for itself.

According to a Swedish businessman who has started several companies in the United States, "Marketing in the U.S. is seen as an investment; to a Swedish company it is more likely to be seen as an expense."

Consensus Rules

Reaching consensus is usually very important to Swedes, even though it can be a time-consuming process that American businesspeople consider inefficient. Any American who has worked for a Swedish company has probably been baffled by the overriding concern for consensus in decision making. In the United States, where individual power is sought after and corporate structures are relatively hierarchical, decisions are typically made at the top and trickle downward for implementation. In Sweden, on the other hand, where organizations are usually flatter and individual power is less prominent, decisions are preferably arrived at using the consensus model.

"In my heart, I was and still am convinced it's a better way of doing things," said Marc Bünger. As an American married to a Swede and who lived in Sweden for five years, he often finds himself the liaison between two cultures. He explained the process of consensus decision making in an interview with one of the authors in late 2000.

"When making a decision to achieve consensus, a Swedish manager will go around the room [to solicit] opinions in turn," he said. "Then, if satisfied, he will summarize with, 'It sounds like we will do X.' And everyone leaves knowing what to do and will get it started."

Leading a decision-making meeting in the United States, the same Swedish manager might follow the same procedure: solicit opinions and summarize. Only the Americans won't understand that a decision has been reached, Bünger noted. "They'll come back to next week's meeting and won't have done anything. Instead they'll wonder, 'Why won't this guy tell us what to do?'" The solution: a compromise. The Swedish manager may still canvass the room for opinions. But in the end, he or she could make specific assignments, Bünger suggested. "He might say, 'Sally, could you do this by Tuesday? Joe, could you take care of that by Friday?' That tells the Americans that a decision was made and that there are things to do."

An American manager making an important decision will not necessarily discuss it with a group or ask everyone's opinion. And if there is discussion, it will most likely be unstructured. "Americans expect people to argue. A good managerial tactic in the U.S. is to say something you don't believe to be true but that will spark discussion," Bünger noted. "People don't go around in turn." But a Swede would be uncomfortable with this management style, he said. "He would think, 'We have a deep rift here,' whereas in the American's eyes, this is simply a natural part of decision making."

To the Swedes consensus means that everyone on the team is involved and buys into decisions. If someone is left out, consensus hasn't truly been reached.

In the Swedes' view, taking the time to reach consensus up front results in quicker progress later, because fewer adjustments will need to be made along the way. Because Swedes are more likely to choose this careful approach over speed, they are less likely to be concerned with the length of the decision-making process. On the contrary, they consider a decision made in haste to be an act of poor judgment.

This can be a source of great frustration for non-Swedes who neither understand nor appreciate why it is necessary to reach full consensus—as opposed to a simple majority, for example—when there is an obvious need for quick action. Although consensus is often perceived as a worthy goal, it may not be viewed as essential. Reaching rapid decisions is considered vital in the United States, where it is essential to stay competitive and where speed equals competitive advantage.

"Most American businesspeople are uncomfortable about the need to reach consensus—if it comes easily, it's fine, but not if it takes too long," said an American executive who worked in Sweden for nearly two decades. "In its best form, the extra time built into the consensus model gives people a chance to think about what they believe. It alleviates haggling and creates a better team spirit. It also provides a way forward to implement the decision that has been reached."

But problems and frustration—felt even by Swedes—can

result when the process becomes hopelessly deadlocked and consensus cannot easily be reached. "You have to know when to stop," the American executive said. There is also a danger that a false consensus may be reached, leading to hidden obstacles down the road. When that happens, it is difficult to correct faulty decisions. "You have to create a crisis and start over to achieve a whole new consensus," said an American business development manager with a Swedish-owned multinational company.

Compared with the more formal way of voting on a decision, which is customary in the United States, an agreement among a group of Swedes is often communicated much more subtly by a combination of slight nods, "mms," and eye contact. Robert Shuter, an expert on cross-cultural communication, points out that because Americans often miss these subtle cues, they are often taken by surprise and assume the Swedes "pulled a fast one."

An American, a member of a technology team composed of mostly Swedes and a few Americans, attended a meeting in Stockholm conducted in English and Swedish. He felt comfortable during the meeting and thought he understood everything that was going on, that is, until the meeting was about to conclude, and he realized that an important decision had been reached without his awareness! He could not figure out how this had happened. There was no vote! No wonder Swedes sometimes leave others scratching their heads (Shuter 1998).

Getting Things Done

It may be easier to understand the Swedish consensus model if you understand Swedes' belief in careful, thorough planning before taking action. Americans frequently complain that Swedes are slow to respond to challenges. A major reason for this is the difference in the ways the two cultures allocate time for planning and action.

According to some estimates, Swedes spend about 50 percent of their time planning, while Americans, on average, devote only about 15 percent of theirs. Imagine two time lines placed next to one another. The U.S. time line shows 15 to 20 percent given to planning and 85 percent devoted to implementation (i.e., action). The Swedish time line, on the other hand, shows 50 percent for both planning and implementation. It is easy to understand how this can cause problems.

When the Americans have finished their planning, they are eager to move forward, with adjustments and detours along the way to deal with any unforeseen obstacles. Putting out fires is part of doing business—at least they're moving forward, making progress. To them the Swedes seem maddeningly slow at this point. However, once the Swedes reach the 50 percent mark, they become the frustrated ones; now they are ready to act and move quickly toward their goal, while the Americans continue to make adjustments, like a missile in search of a target. The Americans find the Swedish style of planning time-consuming and overly cautious; the Swedes find the American style of "shooting from the hip" unreliable and inefficient.

They are, as we can see, simply looking at the situation from different perspectives. The Swedes prefer the lengthy planning stage, looking for all possible obstacles and trying to find ways to avoid future surprises, while the Americans prefer to move ahead and adjust their course as they go. Thus, Swedes are frustrated when they ask American counterparts for details only to be told, "Don't worry; everything will work out." And Americans find it irritating that the Swedes are never satisfied with their rationale during the implementation process.

An American software engineer working in Sweden described her experience with Swedish planning this way:

> Projects take a long time to move from the "design and analysis" phase to the "implementation" phase. Everything

has to be reviewed by many people and agreed upon. If there is not agreement, meetings and investigations and additional research are needed. Perhaps the end product is better, since everything is thought through more thoroughly, but I often wish there was one person who could break the deadlock on an issue so we could just move forward.

If there were one person in the group who could take that step, he or she could be difficult to identify, at least based on appearance. The "boss" is usually dressed just like the rest of the staff, which is often quite casual. Moreover, even if you did manage to find the boss, he or she would probably be reluctant to force a decision and instead work until everyone came to an agreement.

But the American software engineer goes on to say that at her Swedish husband's company, which is quite a bit smaller, things seem to move faster. This may also be an indication of a new trend spurred by Sweden's dominant IT industry. Global competition requires faster reaction times, and countries such as Sweden are struggling to learn to get things done more rapidly.

Flat Organizational Structure

With a de-emphasis on individual competition and a preference for consensus decision making, it would make sense that the Swedish management style reflect these inclinations. It does; in fact one of the most publicized differences between the Swedish and American business styles is the relative lack of hierarchy in Swedish organizations. This is particularly noticeable (and problematic) to people from cultures where authority is important and where position and status within a company are clearly defined, such as France, Germany, the United Kingdom, Japan, and the United States.

Unlike in these countries, where corporations tend to be organized top-down, in Sweden corporate structure tends to be decentralized, with few levels of management. Much less weight is placed on titles and status within the organization. Instead of developing complex, hierarchical reporting structures, Swedish corporations rely more on informal controls among employees at all levels. The Swedes go to a great deal of effort to avoid forcing employees on lower rungs to defer to those higher up. In many companies the flat-management ethic is accomplished literally by physically placing managers and employees on the same floor—remember Jantelagen and equality: no one is better than anyone else.

A Canadian American who has lived in Sweden many years spoke of the "Rule of Coffee." According to this unwritten rule, the highest-ranking person in a group will often fetch the coffee, not the secretary or assistant. Even though this may not be the case at every company, it is not uncommon, and it provides an illustration of how employees in a higher position attempt to minimize status barriers. One author wrote, "Many Swedish businessmen have confused their foreign counterparts because they, as a rule, maintain a low profile and give an impression of being humble and reserved, while, at the same time, having great power" (Rabe 1992, 35). So why does the flat organizational structure work so well in Sweden, and why is it so difficult to blend with the American one?

As discussed in chapter 5, on independence and autonomy, Swedes are raised according to the idea that the individual derives a strong sense of security and strength from being part of a group. One reason why the Swedish management style works is its emphasis on teamwork. Unfortunately, many Swedish managers have found it difficult to produce the same level of teamwork in the United States because the idea of working as a team conflicts with the American ideals of individualism and competition. They complain that someone on the team always prefers to follow his or her own agenda or, worse, competes against other team members.

Consider this hypothetical scenario: Jim, an American, is working for a Swedish-owned company on a project team with mostly Swedish team members. He is used to working in a competitive corporate environment, where to get ahead it is critical that he be noticed. He has also learned that information is power and should not always be shared with everybody.

As the project gets under way, Jim begins to see areas where improvements can be made and decides to use this to his professional advantage. Rather than sharing his observations right away, he waits for an opportunity to impress his manager. It does not take long for Jim's team members to sense that Jim seems to have his own agenda, and they wonder what he is up to. They are not sure they can trust him because he seems to be holding something back, and this unsettles the Swedes. When Jim finally does share his idea, he does so in a group meeting, where he emphasizes how he has been working (on his own) to come up with this great plan.

But Jim's performance does not meet with the praise and admiration he expected. There is a brief acknowledgment that his idea may have merit; then the meeting shifts to another topic. Jim, who had hoped to make a great impression, feels frustrated and undervalued; the Swedes, team members and management alike, feel frustrated because Jim has behaved in a way they find self-serving—he is not a team player. No one is a winner here—not Jim, the team, not the company. The cultural gulf widens a bit.

The "Collaborative" Manager

In the teamwork model, the role of the Swedish manager differs from that of most American managers. Swedish management expert Lena Zander describes the Swedish management role as "constructive co-operation and collaborative coaching" (1998, 4). She traces this style back to the 1930s and the beginning of the Swedish Model, which, as discussed in chapter 2, was characterized by cooperation between capital and labor, including the long-standing belief in collective bargaining. Its roots, though, may stretch as far back as the Vikings, as recounted in chapter 1, and the ship where "we are all equal."

The attitude of employees toward managers is thus also different. Employees expect managers to guide them as needed and to be there for support. They usually recognize managers as having a certain expertise but not necessarily being "better than" or necessarily "knowing more than" the other employees. Authority is acquired through competence and experience, and outward displays of "power" are not encouraged.

"There is a suspicious whiff of political correctness about it all," said an American working for a Stockholm-based corporation, when a manager is "never allowed to say that he or she is a manager" (an exaggeration on the American's part). But it is often easier for Americans to adjust to the flat Swedish system than for Swedes to adjust to the American model, he continued:

> I remember seeing the reactions of an office full of Swedes when, in the middle of a management transition, a new American manager put a transparency on an overhead projector. It was a standard, pyramid-shaped organization chart, showing the new organization. After the meeting, one by one the Swedes slipped into the managing director's office to cry on her shoulder because they were afraid the American manager was going to turn the office into a labor camp. "We don't have managers here!" went the collective cry. The fact that he used a hierarchical way to describe the new office caused huge conflicts. The situation just got worse after that.

This reaction no doubt stems from the fact that Swedish workers, in general, do not like to be supervised. In fact in a large cross-cultural management study, "The Licence to Lead" (Zander 1997), employees in the Scandinavian countries reported the lowest preference for supervision.

The common assumption is that if you have the qualifications for a certain job, you should be able to do it without someone checking up on you. Because this is the expectation of both the employer and employee, there is an unspoken understanding: if asked to have something done at a certain time, the employee should be able to deliver without being reminded. A manager who believed it necessary to supervise in order to maintain control would appear not to trust the employee and thus would not be considered a good manager.

In the United States, on the other hand, a good manager is expected to check in with employees regularly and offer encouragement. A Swedish manager at an IKEA store in the United States experienced this difference firsthand. She began managing her new American employees as she had managed in Sweden, giving them "freedom with responsibility" and not treating them "like children," as she described it, by telling them how to do their jobs. But this approach did not have the expected results. She found that her supervisory style led to employees working less and, in fact, taking advantage of her absence. The Americans, on the other hand, said they didn't know how to respond to a manager who didn't check on their progress or tell them they were doing a good job. Like other foreigners working for Swedes, they tended to interpret the Swedish hands-off management style as indifference or even dislike on the part of the manager—she never gave them any encouragement or acknowledged their efforts with compliments.

The nondirective relationship between managers and employees makes sense in the context of Swedish society and its particular ideas on equality. Thus, the very thing that made Swedish workers insecure—direct supervision and hands-on management—made American workers feel the most secure.

Comparing Swedish and American performance reviews also reveals cultural differences in the relationship between managers and employees. Performance reviews in the United States tend to focus on what employees contribute to the company and whether they met their stated goals. In Sweden performance reviews center on the needs of the individual employee and what can be done for the individual's professional development. This approach can seem oddly "touchy-feely" to Americans used to a more objective approach. In fact an American on assignment in Sweden expressed her discomfort with these reviews, saying that she felt like she was attending some kind of therapy session. She felt that there was too much focus on her personal needs and not enough on recognition for what she had done.

Promotions and salary increases are another area of difference. The salary gap between different jobs is much smaller in Sweden than in the United States—something that has caused some entrepreneurial Swedes to seek their fortunes in the U.S. and elsewhere. In general Swedes are less likely than their American counterparts to focus on promotions and salary increases as motivational factors; similarly, performance reviews are also unlikely to center on them.

Open Communication Channels

Communication between employees and managers is a two-way street in Sweden. Swedish employees are used to being well-informed participants in their companies. So when a traditional American corporation takes over a Swedish one, culture shock can ensue.

When American pharmaceutical company Upjohn & Co. and Swedish pharmaceutical company Pharmacia merged in 1995 to create Pharmacia USA, the aftermath was not pretty. The new business structure, in which the decisions came down from the combined company's New Jersey headquarters, was not popular with the Swedish employees. Some were upset because they felt like they were viewed only "as a resource that should generate the best possible profit" (Kantor 1999). Others complained that they had gone from a culture where management listened to them and held joint discussions to find the best solutions to one where instructions were dictated from headquarters and employees were merely expected to carry them out, without any participation. Of course, it can be equally confusing for Americans when Swedes take over the management of an American company. Communication among management levels is more open in most Swedish companies than is considered the norm in U.S. companies. For example, if an employee needs information and deems it more efficient to bypass his or her immediate supervisor and go to someone else in the company, it is acceptable to do so. In a flat-management organization, there is not the same attachment to position or need to guard one's turf as in the United States. With less emphasis on individual competition and more on equality, the Swede feels comfortable in judiciously bypassing the hierarchical levels of the organization that do exist. Conversely, since they are not as focused on looking out for "number one," managers are less likely to worry about employees "going over their head." The potential for chaos this could cause within a U.S. organization, where outshining or bypassing the boss could be professional suicide, is obvious.

In Sweden employees are expected to suggest improvements and point out if something is not right. In other words it is considered normal for an employee to give advice to his or her manager. Employees are not worried that this will get them in trouble; they see it as their right and responsibility.

However, many people from other cultures, including the United States, are not used to giving unsolicited advice to their superiors—nor are their managers used to receiving it— and managers may be offended or threatened by this relationship. In fact, one of the major problems Swedish managers report about their American subordinates is getting them to speak candidly. It's an unusual role reversal—the usually talkative American reduced to silence before the usually quiet Swede.

"In the U.S., employees defer to the boss, at least in public," Bünger noted. "They may grumble to themselves, but when they hear a manager say something, they assume that's how things will be from now on." A Swedish manager, on the other hand, may float half-formed ideas, expecting feedback from employees. If he works with an American staff, he may be waiting a long time: those who agree with him assume it is a fait accompli; those who disagree with him will not confront him. Meanwhile, if no one objects, even in private, the manager assumes everything is fine.

The Language of Business

As we discussed in chapter 10, Swedish communication styles can be very subtle and difficult for the uninitiated to read. The following, then, is a review of Swedish communication characteristics likely to be encountered in business situations, which we hope will be of help to the non-Swede.

- Because Swedish is a very literal and direct language, Swedes tend to speak English the same way, offering few compliments and embellishments, which are often considered superfluous in Swedish. Swedes often state their opinions bluntly, but they may withhold their opinions if they sense that an argument will arise.

- To the Swede it is more important to be credible than to make an impression. Only promise what you can deliver. Understate rather than overstate.

- Because of Sweden's relatively flat social and business hierarchies, Swedes take the same direct approach with everybody. Saying no to one's manager is not uncommon, nor is it considered out of place.

- Subtle signals such as nods and looks often convey meaning.

- Being a good listener is considered an asset. Silence often means a Swede is analyzing what was said and formulating a response. A vague response from a Swede may mean that he or she needs more time to reflect. In this instance, yes might mean only "Yes, I understand what you are saying."

• It is impolite to interrupt others. Everyone expects to have a chance to voice an opinion.

• Swedes generally smile less often and are not as prone to kid around at work. They tend to separate work and social activities and prefer to focus mainly on business while at work. This does not mean they don't like you!

• When Swedes speak Swedish among themselves, it is usually to clarify something. They will usually be willing to speak English if you ask them to.

• The ability to remain calm and avoid confrontations is a valued character trait. Losing your temper or raising your voice may be interpreted as a lack of self-control and can result in a loss of respect.

Of course, many of the Swedes you meet doing business today may seem quite different from those we have discussed in this chapter, at least by degrees. The fact is, people who have lived or worked abroad tend to be more flexible and open to change, thanks to exposure to new ways of thinking and behaving—one of the finest benefits of traveling and learning about other cultures. But, like the zebra's stripes, our own cultural programming never disappears completely.

Conclusion: Full Speed Ahead

> For even as Sweden, like many countries in Western Europe, is
> continuing to preserve traditional European social programs, it
> has also been embracing entrepreneurship and unrestricted compe-
> tition.
> —Edmund L. Andrews, New York Times, 1999

When we began writing this book, Sweden was emerging
from a deep economic recession that had lasted through much
of the 1990s. Unemployment had been higher than at any
time in recent history, and the Swedish welfare system faced
an uncertain future. At the beginning of the new millennium, however, Sweden's prospects once again look bright,
thanks to det IT-undret (the IT "miracle"). Between 1993 and
1999, the IT sector was responsible for one-third of the
nation's productivity increases and one-fourth of its gross
national product, according to a government report issued in
early 2001 (TT News Service, Jan. 17).

That growth, accompanied by some economic interven-
tions and cuts in social benefits, has helped bolster the Swedish economy. Once again, the world is taking notice of this
odd country that seems to defy so many economic laws, lend-
ing support to its claims that capitalism with a humanitarian
focus is the best model.

171

Although thriving, Sweden still faces many challenges, including reducing taxes while ensuring economic growth and the social welfare of Swedish citizens; addressing immigration issues and learning to function as a multicultural society; embracing globalization and adapting to changes brought about by the IT boom and entrance into the EU; and adjusting to the new values held by the younger generation. At the time of this writing, it appears that Sweden has once again successfully found equilibrium, a middle ground (lagom lives!) between capitalism and the social welfare of folkhemmet.

Taxes and the Economy. During the worldwide recession of the early 1990s, Swedes were more divided than usual in determining the direction their country should take to turn things around. On one side, the Social Democrats and other left-leaning parties continued to espouse the ideals of the Swedish Model with its broad social safety net. On the other side, the *Moderaterna* (only in Sweden would the "conservative" party be called the Moderates) and other right-wing parties sought lower taxes and a more competitive market economy.

The formula for success included cutting or modifying some social benefits, deregulating the electricity and telecom industries, and easing some labor regulations. Along with some judiciously targeted tax increases, these measures had a noticeable effect within just a few years. Entrepreneurship has grown remarkably since the mid-1990s, and Sweden currently has one of Europe's strongest economies, its IT sector rivaling even that of the United States.

The economic turnaround came at a price, however. Swedish voters, distrustful of politics and the political system after years of unemployment, turned out in record-low numbers for the 1998 election; only about 80 percent voted. (That would be astonishingly high for an American election, but for the Swedes, it was nothing to boast about.) The Social Democrats, who had displeased voters by cutting some social benefits, did not garner enough votes to claim a majority government; instead, they were forced to form a coalition with the Left and Green Parties.

Sweden will likely continue to grapple with its costly social system and consider cutting taxes to stimulate economic growth. Although taxes and labor-protection laws may discourage some foreign companies from opening offices in Sweden, the nation's humming economy and position as a major IT player have convinced many U.S. companies to suspend their concerns and open regional offices in Sweden. Some Swedes fear that an economic downturn could induce some large Swedish companies to move headquarters abroad and encourage the nation's best and brightest to find greener pastures elsewhere. For now, however, Sweden is enjoying an influx of talent and industry.

Unemployment. Unemployment in Sweden is under control, but the economic tumult of the 1990s and ensuing unemployment—13 percent at one point—frightened the Swedes with a labor scare they had not experienced in seventy years. Most Swedes believed a job would always be available; employment was practically guaranteed.

Employment trends in Sweden now mirror those in the United States. Labor regulations have changed to permit temporary employment (previously illegal under union laws), and placement agencies are thriving. Young people are less likely than their parents to seek lifetime employment in large corporations or with the public sector, but instead they go where opportunities take them. With deregulation and more opportunities to start their own businesses, many Swedes are opting to become freelancers and entrepreneurs, leaving Jantelagen in their wake. By many accounts, Sweden is becoming a true hotbed for start-ups.

The Welfare Machine. Social benefits were pruned during the 1990s with considerable resistance. It is never easy to give up what one has become accustomed to having. At the same time, it had become clear that Sweden's costly system was something of an albatross. The Swedes remain commit-ted to the philosophy that a government should ensure the welfare of all its citizens and guarantee that no one falls between the cracks. But even Sweden has found this easier said than done. Like many other European countries with extensive social programs, Sweden continues to seek ways to maintain its social safety net, including health care, educa-tion, and state-guaranteed vacations, among other benefits. Taxes in Sweden are among the highest in the world. They are tolerated because most people still consider what they receive in social services to be worth the cost.

Another factor that will play an increasingly important role in making social welfare decisions is demographics. Swe-den has the highest percentage in Europe of people over the age of 80. At the same time, population growth due to new births is decreasing. The question is, who will be around to pay for the welfare system in the future?

Immigration. Immigration to Sweden has slowed somewhat since the 1970s and 1980s, and residency requirements have become more stringent. However, with a substantial portion of Swedes now first- or second-generation immigrants, the country continues to grapple with issues of integration and remains ambivalent about its new status as an ethnic melting pot.

Sweden attracted many immigrants because of its policy, based on a strong sense of humanitarian responsibility, to offer a haven to victims of political persecution. Despite good intentions, some programs that were supposed to help new-comers have instead caused them additional problems.

Immigrant populations have become segregated geographi-cally in areas where economic conditions tend to be poorer. The immigrant label is also difficult to shake. Anyone born to immigrant parents or newly arrived in Sweden is likely to be lumped into the general category of "immigrant," not because of discrimination but as a result of efforts to ensure that all immigrants receive the protection of antidiscrimination laws and other special accommodations afforded by the Swedish government. Unfortunately, the insistence on labeling and treating immigrants as a subgroup perpetuates differences rather than promoting integration—resulting in societal marginalization.

Many immigrants seem to understand that the Swedish government means well, but they are frustrated nevertheless. In an article in *Dagens Nyheter* titled "Vi vill hejda den välvilliga rasismen" ("We Want to Stop This Well-Intentioned Racism"), young people from immigrant families made it clear that although they know why it occurs, the practice of classifying individuals such as themselves as immigrants must eventually stop (Albons 2000).

Sweden is still learning how to function as a multicultural society. Even its best efforts to promote diversity and integration leave room for improvement. It may take another generation or more to accept new Swedes as truly Swedish and make them feel a real part of Swedish society.

Globalization and the European Union. As we have discussed throughout this book, Sweden has a long history of international contacts. Multinational corporations such as Ericsson, ABB, and Electrolux continue to operate globally, while smaller companies as well have steadily begun to expand internationally.

As a result, Swedish companies are learning how to blend their beliefs and management styles with those of local markets—not always an easy task. They must accept that their ways are not always considered best and show a willingness to adapt and be flexible in order to succeed. Sweden does have an advantage in that most of its citizens speak some English, and many speak one or more additional languages.

Sweden has been a member of the European Union since 1995. The country was more reluctant to join the EU than many other European nations have been, and even in current opinion polls, approval rates of EU membership vacillate. Although it joined the EU, Sweden chose to remain outside the European Monetary Fund, a choice that may or may not be reversed in the near future by a Swedish popular vote. Swedish resistance to the EU and the Euro can be attributed largely to the belief that by following the rules and regulations set by EU, many advantages of living in Sweden will be lost. (Although, as we have noted, many Swedes welcome the relaxation of Sweden's alcohol policy.)

In the summer of 2000, a bridge between Sweden and Denmark, Öresundsbron, was officially opened, connecting Sweden for the first time to mainland Europe. Today, the new bridge/tunnel combination makes it possible to drive all the way from northern Sweden to Italy, psychologically making Sweden feel a bit less removed and more connected to the continent.

Sweden, which has long enjoyed close ties to Estonia, Latvia, and Lithuania, has become a launching pad for businesses in the Baltic States because companies wishing to reach these countries as well as others in Eastern Europe have found Sweden to be an excellent base of operations.

The Younger Generation. Today's young Swedes seem well prepared for the global economy. Most have traveled to some foreign destination through international student-exchange programs, on sabbatical, or simply for pleasure. In addition, a very high percentage of young people have Internet access, and consequently their worldview is changing in many ways.

Young Swedes today are likely to demand more from a job than their parents did and are less likely than previous generations to remain with one company. "Am I loyal to my company? Sorry to disappoint, but, no!" said one Swede. "I am loyal to some of the people within the company. I have even worked in companies where I have shown loyalty to my boss, but, at the end of the day, my only loyalty is to myself" (*Sweden Today* 2000, 26).

The views of this individual, a young entrepreneur in the new digital economy, may not represent the views of all young Swedes, but changes are definitely occurring. On the surface, at least, it seems that young Swedes are becoming more individualistic and less constrained by the strict perimeters of Jantelagen. With increased exposure to other cultures, some Swedish reserve is breaking down. Swedes who have studied or worked abroad will tell you that they feel more open and receptive than friends without the same experience.

The IT Explosion. "Who says entrepreneurs always go where the taxes are low? Sweden, where income taxes are among the highest in Europe, has become the continent's hottest market for Internet startups, by some measures hotter than America" (Invest in Sweden Agency 2000).

American technology futurist Paul Saffo calls Sweden "the most advanced consumer test-bed on the planet—far ahead of the rest of Europe and the United States"—in the fields of wireless applications and broadband technology (McGuire 2000, 3).

These achievements are not bad for a country of fewer than nine million people. Articles in major magazines in Europe and the United States highlight Sweden as one of the most wired and wireless countries in the world. Sweden is looking increasingly attractive to many American high-tech companies in spite of its steep personal income taxes and less-than-ideal geographic location.

In the brave new world of initial public offerings and hot Internet stocks, Sweden is also in the forefront, which may seem to contradict the preferences for risk aversion and slow decision making that we talked about in this book. We have seen other sides of the Swedish character as well, however, such as practicality, a reliance on reason and logic, and a focus on quality. And don't forget Sweden's history of engineering and innovation. Today, all of these factors have come together, resulting in high-energy expansion. Although cautious in many ways—sensible and pragmatic, the Swedes might prefer to call themselves—they have no fear of new technology. The Swedes embraced the telephone one hundred years ago; today six in ten own a mobile phone (second only to Finland in mobile-phone penetration), and more than five in ten use the Internet. To help produce a workforce skilled in the latest technologies, IT universities are cropping up around the country.

Just as inventions made around the turn of the last century led to the creation of so many of Sweden's large multinational corporations, perhaps what we are seeing now is the birth of a new generation of "genius firms," poised to lead Sweden into its next modern phase.

The World's Conscience. Because of its strong humanitarian orientation, Sweden has frequently been referred to as the world's conscience; this is not always meant as a compliment, nor is it likely to change. The Swedes' conviction that their model of democracy is ideal in many ways leads them to find models in many other countries—including the United States—lacking. The Swedes are quite aware of their idiosyncrasies, however, and are not above a little self-mockery (although they are more sensitive when the criticism comes from outsiders).

"The world has now realized Sweden's unique position," wrote Rickard Fuchs in his tongue-in-cheek *Visst är det härligt att vara svensk* (*It Sure Is Wonderful to Be Swedish*).

> If you sit high up in the bleachers at a soccer game, you have a very good view. You have a perfect view of the playing field and the players and can therefore see things the players themselves cannot see. Due to this fact, you can from this position in the bleachers see how the game actually ought to be played. Abroad they have understood that it is the same thing with Sweden and the world. Because Sweden is positioned high up in the bleachers, far from the center of the events, we in Sweden have a perfect view of the world and can see how the world ought to be managed.... We can sit at the top of the bleachers with binoculars and tell what is wrong in other countries, located very far away from us. (1991, 151–52)

Indeed, Sweden is already quite vocal about sharing its opinions on the North Atlantic Treaty Organization (NATO), an alliance it seems increasingly likely to want to join. A U.S. official in Brussels noted that the Swedes "may be newcomers to the club, but that doesn't stop them from having ideas about how we could do almost everything better if we only listened to Swedish thinking."

Based on sometimes limited or one-sided information, the Swedes can be very upset by what they perceive to be unfair treatment of minorities and people in need in the United States. There is a sense of incomprehension that such a wealthy country does not take better care of its people. These sentiments are well-intentioned and not unlike the American outrage at human rights violations around the world. The difference is a matter of degree and perspective.

But Sweden does act in accordance with its criticisms: its per capita foreign developmental aid, although somewhat lower during the economic downturn of the 1990s, remains among the highest in the world, and it is constantly looking for new ways to help. One group that is beginning to attract interest among Swedes from different political backgrounds and diverse walks of life is the Association for the Taxation of Financial Transactions for the Relief of Citizens (ATTAC). Founded in France, ATTAC promotes the Tobin Tax, a tax on currency transactions on foreign exchange markets that could create revenue for basic environmental and human needs. Participation in these kinds of global efforts may be one way for the Swedes to demonstrate their humanitarian zeal without being viewed as the world's self-imposed moral policemen.

Swedish Views on the United States. Sweden may be one of the most Americanized countries in the world, but that doesn't prevent Swedes from openly sharing what they find wrong with American culture. As one of the authors once wrote, Swedes seem to think "everything about America is terrible except for the music, movies, TV, sports, clothes, language, and food" (Carr 1991, 5).

The Swedes laud aspects of American culture of which they approve (e.g., new technology) while criticizing, as mentioned above, perceived injustices and excesses. Critics often target what they view as American cultural hegemony. Swedes are not alone in criticizing American culture, of course; many countries feel an acute need to protect their cultural identity, while at the same time satisfying curiosity regarding outside influences. This struggle is certain to continue as the Swedes evolve as both a multicultural and a global society.

In January 2000 the Swedish Institute for North American Studies launched a study aimed at exploring and clarifying American influences on Sweden. This comprehensive study, to be completed in four years, will examine how American cultural elements are adopted into Swedish culture and how they take on new meaning through this process.

In Sweden's journey from Viking stronghold to strong, modern society, the Swedish Model has not reached the end of the long road. With its engineering tradition enjoying new life, its strong egalitarian spirit unbroken, and its deep-seated belief that everything would be right with the world if only reason and pragmatism prevailed intact, Sweden continues its journey into the twenty-first century full speed ahead. In a country with lagom in its genes, finding a life of perfect balance for its people seems to be an eternal quest.

Bibliography

Åberg, Alf. 1985. *A Concise History of Sweden*. Stockholm: LTs Förlag.

Ahlbeck, Cecilia. 1998. *Metro*. March 27. URL: www.metro.se/daily.980327/html

Albons, Birgitta. 2000. "Vi Vill Hejda den Välvilliga Rasismen." *Dagens Nyheter*, November 13.

Anders, John. 1992. "Where Life Is Swede and Pricey." *Dallas Morning News*, April 12.

Andersson, Bengt. 1993. *Swedishness*. Stockholm, Sweden: Positive Sweden.

Andrews, Edmund L. 1999. "Rebounding Sweden Defies the Laws of Economic Gravity." *New York Times*, October 8.

Åsard, Erik, Elisabeth Herion-Sarafidids, and Dag Blanck. 1999. "American Influences in Sweden." Application submitted to the Faculty of Languages, Uppsala University, March 1. URL: www.sinas.uu.se/aminfl.htm

Austin, Paul Britten. 1968. *On Being Swedish: Reflections towards a Better Understanding of the Swedish Character*. London: Martin Secker & Warburg.

Beckman, Birger. 1946. *Lasternas Bok: Våra Kulturfel*. Stockholm: Bokförlaget Natur och Kultur.

181

Belt, Don. 1993. "Sweden: In Search of a New Model." *National Geographic*. August, 2–35.

Benson, Anders. 1998. "Workplace Quality: Another Office Oxymoron!" *Currents*. Swedish-American Chamber of Commerce, February.

Berlin, Peter. 1994. *The Xenophobe's Guide to the Swedes*. London: Ravette Books.

Board, Joseph B. 1995. "Sweden: A Model Crisis." *Current Sweden*, no. 410. The Swedish Institute. Stockholm.

Britton, Claes. 1999. *Sweden and the Swedes*. Stockholm: The Swedish Institute.

Bünger, Marc. 2000. Interview. December 20.

Carr, Lisa Werner. 1991. "The American Emigrant." *Nordstjernan*, May 2.

Childs, Marquis. 1947. *Sweden: The Middle Way*. 1980. Reprint, New Haven, CT: Yale University Press.

Curle, David. 1997, 1998, 1999. Interviews. November 20, January 4, and September 29.

Dahlbom-Hall, Barbro. 1999. "The Boys Are in Charge." *Nordstjernan*, February 18.

Dahlström, Eva. 1997. *Möten med Sverige*. Stockholm: Kulturdepartementet.

Daun, Åke. 1996. *Swedish Mentality*. University Park: Pennsylvania State University Press.

Davies, Norman. 1996. *Europe: A History*. Oxford, England: Oxford University Press.

Elstob, Eric. 1979. *Sweden: A Political and Cultural History*. Lanham, MD: Rowan & Littlefield.

Erlander, Tage. 1972. *Tage Erlander: 1901–1939*. Stockholm: Tidens Förlag.

Fahlman, Gösta. 1999. "The Vasa Ship: Sweden's Treasure and Tourist Attraction." *Vasa Star*, January–February.

Fitchett, Joseph. 1998. "With Popular Opinion Pro-NATO, Neutral Sweden Warms to Alliance." *International Herald Tribune*, January 30.

Franklin, Benjamin. 1733. *Poor Richard's Almanac.*

Frykman, Jonas, and Orvar Löfgren. 1991. *Svenska vanor och ovanor.* Stockholm: Bokförlaget Natur och Kultur.

Fuchs, Rickard. 1991. *Visst är det härligt att vara svensk.* Stockholm: Wahlström & Widstrand.

Gannon, Martin J., and Associates. 1994. *Understanding Global Cultures: Metaphorical Journeys through Seventeen Countries.* Thousand Oaks, CA: Sage Publications.

Gaunt, David, and Orvar Lofgren. 1984. *Myterna om Svensken.* Stockholm: Liber Förlag.

Gramstad, Borghild. 1997. "Janteloven." *Magasinett,* Fall.

Hadénius, Stig, Torbjörn Nilsson, and Gunnar Asélius. 1996. *Sveriges Historia.* Stockholm: Bonnier Alba.

Hagberg, Marie. 1997. "Where Are the Swedish Gentlemen?" *Amelia,* no. 4, February.

Hampden-Turner, Charles, and Alfons Trompenaars. 1993. *The Seven Cultures of Capitalism.* New York: Doubleday.

Heller, Richard. 2000. "Folk Fortune." *Forbes,* September 4.

Herlitz, Gillis. 1991. *Svenskar: Hur är vi och varför vi är som vi är.* Stockholm: Gillis Herlitz and Konsultföretaget AB.

Hofstede, Geert. 1991. *Cultures and Organizations.* London: McGraw-Hill International.

Hoge, Warren. 1998. "Stockholm Journal: In Years since Palme Killing, a Loss of Innocence." *New York Times,* September 1.

Invest in Sweden Agency. 2000. Speaker's notes to "Sweden in Facts & Figures 2000." URL: http://isa.se/slides/facts/notes.htm

Johnsson, Hans-Ingvar. 1995. *Sverige i Fokus.* Stockholm: The Swedish Institute.

Jones, Gwyn. *A History of the Vikings.* 1984. Rev. ed. Oxford, England: Oxford University Press.

Jones, Prudence, and Nigel Pennick. 1995. *A History of Pagan Europe.* New York: Barnes & Noble.

Kantor, Jan. 1999. "Kulturkrock så det barra smäller om det." *Svenska Dagbladet,* February 4.

184

Kisthinios, Kristina. 1996. A Scent of Sweden. Lund, Sweden: Tralala Reklambyra AB.

Laine-Sveiby, Kati. 1987. Svenskhet som strategi. Sweden: Timbro.

Larsson, Lena. 1968. Sweden: A Year. Stockholm: Forums Fackboksredaktion.

Lindqvist, Herman. 1989. Reports from the Land in the Middle. Stockholm: Herman Lindqvist and Sveriges Radios Förlag.

Lönnroth, Ami. 2001. "Vi Tänker Inte Upprepa Föräldragenerationens Misstag." Svenska Dagbladet, January 4. URL: svd.se/dynamiskt/Idag/did_886693.asp

Lövin, Isabella. 1999. "Den Europeiska Modellen." Månadsjournalen, no. 8, August.

Magnusson, Magnus. 1980. Vikings! New York: Elsevier-Dutton.

McGuire, Stryker. 2000. "Shining Stockholm." Newsweek International, February 7.

McIntosh, Bill. 1995. "How to Sell in Scandinavia." Trade & Culture, September/October.

Moliteus, Magnus. 1999. Interview. August 7.

Möller, Tommy. 2001. Interview. April 27.

Nilson, Ulf. 1998. Nordstjernan, 2 July, 7.

Palmer, Brian. 2001. Interview. January 12.

———. 2000. "Wolves at the Door: Existential Solidarity in a Globalizing Sweden." Ph.D. diss., Harvard University.

Phillips-Martinsson, Jean. 1991. Swedes as Others See Them. Lund, Sweden: Studentlitteratur.

Press release. 2000. "Jante tvingas lämna Sollefteå." Sollefteå Kommun, June 20.

Rabe, Monica. 1992. Kulturella Glasögon. Göteborg, Sweden: Tre Böcker Förlag AB.

Rekdal, Lena. 1997. The Newcomer's Practical Handbook for Sweden. Stockholm: DIC.

Rich, Louise Dickinson. 1962. The First Book of Vikings. New York: Franklin Watts.

Sahlin, Mona. 1997. "Trygghet och förändring." Vår Bostad, January.

Sandemose, Aksel. 1972. *En Flyktning Krysser Sine Spor*. Oslo: Den norske bokklubben.

Seelye, H. Ned, and Alan Seelye-James. 1995. *Culture Clash: Managing in a Multicultural World*. Lincolnwood, IL: NTC.

Shuter, Robert. 1998. "Bloopers." *Currents*. Swedish-American Chamber of Commerce, December.

Sonesson, Göran. "In Search of Swedish Nature." URL: http://www.arthist.lu.se/kultsem/sonesson/swed_cult_1.html (Originally published in Polish translation in *Magazyn Sztuki*, no. 8, April 1995).

Statement of Government Policy (unofficial translation) presented by the Prime Minister to Parliament on October 6, 1998. URL: www.regeringen.se/se/regeringen/regeringsforklaring/tidigareregeringsforkl.../980610eng.htm

Statistics Sweden/Statistiska Centralbyrån. 2000. General database. Stockholm. URL: www.scb.se/

Steinberg, John. 1999. Interview. February 15.

Sturmark, Christer. 2000. "Sverige i den Nya Ekonomin." *Svenska Dagbladet*, March 1.

Svensson, Charlotte Rosen. 1996. *Culture Shock: A Guide to Customs and Etiquette in Sweden*. Singapore: Times Editions.

Swahn, Jan-Öjvind. 1994. *Maypoles, Crayfish, and Lucia: Swedish Holidays and Traditions*. Jan-Öjvind Swahn and The Swedish Institute.

Sweden Today. 2000. "Keeping Your Head when All About You...," U.S. ed., no. 2.

The Swedish Institute. 2000a. Fact Sheet on Sweden: Equality Between Women and Men, February. Stockholm.

The Swedish Institute. 2000b. Fact Sheet on Sweden: The Swedish Economy, October. Stockholm.

The Swedish Institute. 1999. Fact Sheet on Sweden: The Swedish Political Parties, April. Stockholm.

The Swedish Institute. 1999. Fact Sheet on Sweden: General Facts on Sweden, April. Stockholm.

The Swedish Institute. 1998. "Sweden, 1998: One Election, Two Realities." *Current Sweden*, no. 420. June. Stockholm.

The Swedish Institute. 1997. Fact Sheet on Sweden: Family Planning in Sweden, June. Stockholm.

The Swedish Institute. 1997. Fact Sheet on Sweden: Alfred Nobel and the Nobel Prizes, October. Stockholm.

Swenson, Karen. 1997. *Greta Garbo: A Life Apart*. New York: Scribner.

Systembolaget. 2000. "Why Should We Have to Suffer for the Sake of a Few Alcoholics? And Seventeen Other Questions." Systembolaget AB.

Uddenberg, Agneta. 1994. *Rätt Sätt*. Stockholm: Wahlström & Widstrand.

———. 1992. *Vett och Etikett på 90-talet*. Västerås, Sweden: ICA Förlaget AB.

Valdemarsson, Bengt. 1997. "Kurs mot Friheten." *Utlandsjuristen*, August 10.

Vesilind, Priit J. 2000. "In Search of Vikings." *National Geographic*, May.

Von Otter, Birgitta. 1998. "New Swedish Government Needs Two Crutches." *Current Sweden*, no. 421. October. The Swedish Institute. Stockholm.

Webster's New World Dictionary of the American Language. 1970. New York: The World Publishing Company.

Weibull, Jorgen. 1993. *Swedish History in Outline*. Stockholm: The Swedish Institute & Wiken Förlags AB.

Wirtén, Per. *Hellre fattig Än Arbetslös*. 1997. Stockholm: Norstedts Förlag AB.

Zander, Lena. 1997. "The Licence to Lead." Ph.D. diss., Institute of International Business, Stockholm School of Economics.

———. 1998. "Management in Sweden." Institute of International Business, Stockholm School of Economics.

Index

188

About the Authors

Christina Johansson Robinowitz is founder of The Cross-Cultural Coach, an intercultural consulting firm, and is a consultant, trainer, and speaker on intercultural issues. Born and raised in Sweden, Christina lives and works in the United States. She has a master's degree in Professional Development with a concentration in intercultural communication and training and specializes in Swedish-U.S. relations.

Lisa Werner Carr, an American of Swedish descent, is a professional journalist and has lived and worked in Sweden. Now based in Dallas, she is a Web content developer and contributing editor to *Sweden & America* magazine.

9 781877 864889